Classic
Cars

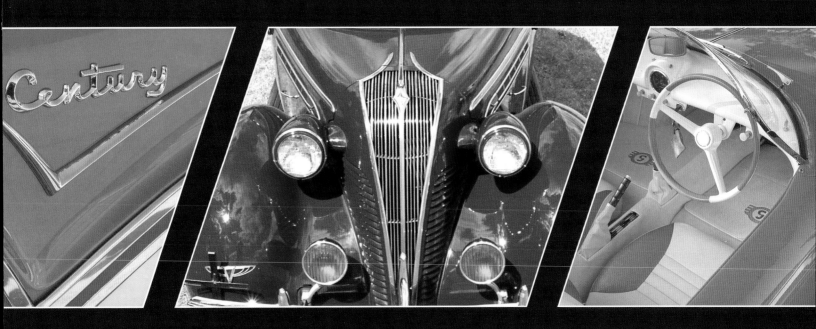

Publications International, Ltd.

Louis Weber, CEO
Publications International, Ltd.
8140 Lehigh Avenue
Morton Grove, IL 60053

Permission is never granted for commercial purposes.

ISBN: 978-1-64558-592-3

Manufactured in China.

8 7 6 5 4 3 2 1

Let's get social!

[instagram] @Publications_International   [facebook] @CollectibleAutomobile

[facebook] @PublicationsInternational   [facebook] @cgautomotive

www.pilbooks.com

CREDITS

We would like to thank the following vehicle owners and photographers for supplying the images in this book.

1913 Chevrolet: O: Sloan Museum; P: Al Rogers. **1926 Ford:** O: J. Norman Gwinn; P: Vince Manocchi. **1927 Velie:** O: Charles Hoaglund; P: Doug Mitchel. **1929 Cadillac:** O: Thomas Tkacz; P: Leigh Dorrington. **1931 Oakland:** O: Tim & Penny Dye; P: Jim White. **1933 Dodge:** O: Stewart Solomon ; P: Vince Manocchi. **1937 Chrysler:** O: Robert Hepler; P: Vince Manocchi. **1937 Hudson:** O: Eldon & Esta Hostetler; P: W.C. Waymack. **1937 Oldsmobile:** O: Warren Danz; P: Doug Mitchel. **1938 Peugeot:** O: Scott Boses & Raymond Milo; P: Neil Nissing. **1939 Ford:** O: Gary & Terri Cambio; P: Vince Manocchi. **1939 Nash:** O: Lloyd Hardy; P: Vince Manocchi. **1940 Plymouth:** O: David Simon; P: David Gooley. **1941 Buick:** O: Jon Greuter; P: Doug Mitchel. **1941 Packard:** O: Neil Torrence; P: Vince Manocchi. **1941 Willys:** O: Al Maynard; P: Doug Mitchel. **1942 Dodge:** O: Don & Britt Feldman; P: Al Rogers. **1942 Pontiac:** O: Raul Shimizu; P: Vince Manocchi. **1947 Triumph:** O: Gary & Junie Cooper; P: David Gooley. **1948 Ford:** O: Bob Massey; P: Doug Mitchel. **1949 Anglia:** O: Douglas & Marlene Munro; P: Richard Spiegelman. **1950 Chevrolet:** O: Jerrold Murphy; P: Brandon Hemphill. **1950 DeSoto:** O: Jim Edwards; P: Vince Manocchi. **1951 Chrysler:** O: Art Astor; P: Vince Manocchi. **1951 Jowett:** O: David Burrows; P: Al Rogers. **1952 Buick:** O: Stephen Shore; P: David Temple. **1952 Healey Tickford:** O: Bryan Williams; P: Nicky Wright. **1952 Packard:** O: Ralph Marano; P: Don Heiny. **1952 Pontiac:** O: Aspen Pittman; P: Vince Manocchi. **1952 Siata:** O: Blackhawk Collection; P: Phil Toy. **1953 Cadillac:** O: Leonard Nagel; P: Vince Manocchi. **1953 Chrysler:** O: John White; P: Phil Toy. **1953 Dannenhauer and Stauss:** O: Dick Christensen; P: David Gooley. **1953 Henry J:** O: Jerry Monterastelli; P: Doug Mitchel. **1953 Mercury:** O: Merrit Johnson; P: David Temple. **1954 Ford:** O: Merle Coile; P: Doug Mitchel. **1954 Studebaker:** O: Malcolm Stinson Jr.; P: Randall Bohl. **1955 Chrysler:** O: John Lazenby; P: David Gooley. **1955 Hudson:** O: Charles Benjamin; P: Vince Manocchi. **1956 DeSoto:** O: Bob Justice; P: Al Rogers. **1956 Ford:** O: John Petras; P: Doug Mitchel. **1956 Maserati:** O: Johnathan Segal; P: David Gooley. **1956 Oldsmobile:** O: Jimmy Blackburn; P: David Temple. **1956 Packard:** O: Ralph & Kathy Tompkins; P: Doug Mitchel. **1957 Buick:** O: Dennis Etcheverry; P: Phil Toy. **1957 Chevrolet:** O: Mike Strand; P: Doug Mitchel. **1957 Ford:** O: Jay Kingston; P: Phil Toy. **1957 Mercedes-Benz:** O: Bob Gunthrop; P: David Gooley. **1959 Buick:** O: Robert & Dolores Olness; P: Phil Toy. **1959 Chevrolet:** O: Kenneth Zander; P: Phil Toy. **1959 Chrysler:** O: John Knab; P: Doug Mitchel. **1959 Goggomobil:** O: Greg & Kiki Hahs; P: David Gooley. **1959 Jaguar:** O: Peter Rothenberg; P: David Gooley. **1959 Mercury:** O: Joe Carfagna; P: Don Heiny. **1959 Oldsmobile:** O: John & Vicki Mayer; P: Doug Mitchel. **1960 Edsel:** O: Judy Doster; P: David Temple. **1960 Ford:** O: Andy Linsky; P: Phil Toy. **1960 Plymouth:** O: Frank Troost; P: Doug Mitchel. **1960 Studebaker:** O: Malcolm Stinson Jr.; P: Randall Bohl. **1961 Chevrolet:** O: Ken Lingenfelter; P: Al Rogers. **1962 Mercury:** O: Gary Richards ; P: Vince Manocchi. **1962 Oldsmobile:** O: Rich Baughman; P: Doug Mitchel. **1962 Pontiac:** O: Michael Jalving; P: Mike Spenner. **1963 Ford:** O: Kenneth Kowalk; P: Al Rogers. **1963 Volkswagen:** O: Kiki Hahs; P: David Gooley. **1964 Ford:** O: Gary Spracklin; P: David Temple. **1964 Rambler:** O: Daniel Griffin; P: Thomas Glatch. **1966 Mercury:** O: Gary Gross; P: Doug Mitchel. **1966 Plymouth:** O: Tyrone Phillips; P: Doug Mitchel. **1966 Volvo:** O: Arnold Quast; P: Jeff Cohn. **1967 BMW:** O: Christian Weissmann; P: Vince Manocchi. **1968 Kaiser Jeep:** O: John Hughes; P: Doug Mitchel. **1970 Jaguar:** O: Don Magargee; P: David Gooley. **1971 Fiat:** O: Carlo Panozzo; P: Doug Mitchel. **1971 Toyota:** O: Joji Luz; P: Vince Manocchi. **1972 AMC:** O: Sue Brown; P: Doug Mitchel. **1972 Oldsmobile:** O: Michael Calhoon; P: Tom Shaw. **1973 Ford:** O: Ramona & Mike Wilson; P: Ken Beebe.

CONTENTS

INTRODUCTION

Welcome to a great and dramatic story. The automotive landscape is rich in color and variety, and in *Classic Cars*, The Editors of Consumer Guide Automotive have searched our photographic archive to share some of our favorites. Think of this book as a scrapbook of sorts where the major and minor, the memorable and the forgettable, come together to help tell the story of the automobile roughly from the period from just before World War I up until the first OPEC oil embargo.

In looking back at the development of the automobile over this time frame, one can't help but note how world events had a hand in shaping its history. World War I prompted engineers to accelerate mechanical technology, advancements that soon found their way into production cars. The Great Depression forced many companies out of business. Soon after, World War II virtually halted development for half a decade or more.

In America, a nationwide recession in 1958 not only helped kill off Packard and newcomer Edsel, it also prompted more widespread acceptance of imports from Europe and eventually Japan along with the resurgence of domestically built economical compacts. Around this same time, "niche" vehicles found commercial success, and this soon led to muscle cars, pony cars, and luxurious personal coupes. The result was an automotive free-for-all, especially in Detroit, where product choice and horsepower seemingly ramped up with no end in sight.

But the line was soon drawn. By the late 1960s, government safety regulations were playing a growing role in automotive design, and these standards also set further barriers of entry for independent automakers and off-the-beaten-path imports. Then the 1973 OPEC oil embargo changed what had been a rosy picture just five years earlier into one that was decidedly gray.

What a story. We hope you will enjoy reading it as much as we have enjoyed telling it.

The Editors of Consumer Guide Automotive
Morton Grove, Illinois
March 2021

1913 Chevrolet Type C Tourer

The first Chevrolet doesn't seem much like a Chevy. It wasn't reasonably priced or modestly sized. It didn't have an overhead-valve engine. It didn't even wear a bowtie badge.

The Chevrolet Type C, also known as the Classic Six, was the product of two conflicting personalities with some shared history. William Durant was a dealmaker. Fresh from his first ouster from General Motors in 1910, he was ready to establish a new automotive empire. Louis Chevrolet was what we'd now call a "car guy." A winning driver for Buick's racing team when Durant owned the company, he now wanted to design a car of his own. Durant wanted to build a light, inexpensive car; Chevrolet dreamed of a grand machine to proudly bear his name. In 1911, with Durant's backing, Chevrolet started working on a prototype in a Detroit factory. What developed was bigger and more expensive than Durant's vision.

When the Classic Six touring car entered production in late 1912 as a 1913 model, it was powered by a big 299-cid six and rode on a long 120-inch wheelbase. The price was a hefty $2150, and it probably cost more than that to build. However, Louis Chevrolet was justly proud of his car.

The engine was a T-head, which was a side-valve engine with intake and exhaust valves on opposite sides of the cylinder. This arrangement was favored for performance cars of the time. The crankshaft was well balanced and had counterweights so that it ran smoothly. The engine developed 40 bhp, enough to push the 3350-pound car up to 65 mph. The Classic Six was well equipped with electric lighting and a compressed-air starter that eliminated the need for manual cranking.

The speedometer was lighted to ease night driving, and there was a fuel gauge on the dash. Most cars at the time either didn't have a gas gauge or had one on the tank, not in easy view of the driver. The Classic Six was built to last and perhaps that contributed to its substantial weight. Satisfied with his namesake car, Louis Chevrolet left on a trip to his native Switzerland.

While Chevrolet was meticulously developing his ideal car, Durant had been moving much faster to bring popularly priced cars to market. A Little Four (named for William Little, a former Buick general manager) was on

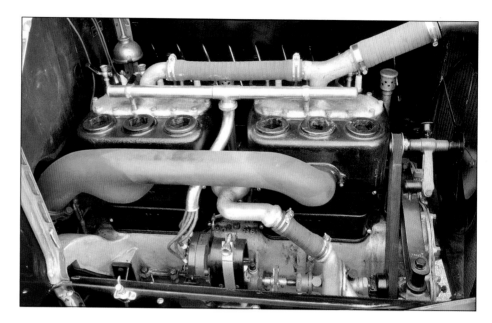

sale in 1912, and a Little Six made its debut at the same time as the Classic Six. When Chevrolet returned from his trip, he discovered that production of the slow-selling Classic Six had been moved from Detroit to the Little plant in Flint, Michigan. What's more, the Little Six became the Chevrolet Special Little Six, and four-cylinder Chevys were on the way. Chevrolet wasn't happy and legend has it that he finally stormed out of the company when Durant told him

to start smoking cigars instead of less-dignified cigarettes.

Classic Six production ended in 1914. Meanwhile, low-cost Chevrolets made Durant rich enough to buy his way back into the leadership of GM in 1915, and established the mass-market brand that we know today.

This Classic Six is the oldest running Chevrolet. It bears body number 323, and was built after Chevrolet's move to the factory in Flint.

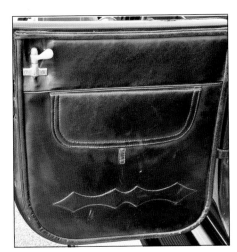

1926 Ford Model T Touring Car

Henry Ford didn't give up easily on his Model T, even though sales and market share were dropping in the mid Twenties. Ford held 50 percent of the market in 1924, but slipped to 44 percent in 1925. Rather than replace a design that had started production in 1908, Henry decided to give his "Universal Car" another chance with an extensive facelift.

The 1926 Fords had a new radiator shell and a longer hood that blended smoothly with the cowl. Fenders were new and running boards were lower. In fact, the whole car was lower. The chassis rode 1.5 inches lower and with lower seats, the height of the touring car was reduced 4.5 inches. Although the wheelbase stood pat at 100 inches, the touring car's body was 3.5 inches longer. One

benefit of the longer and lower Model T was increased interior room with wider seats and more rear legroom.

A choice of colors other than black was available for the first time since 1914. When production of the 1926 models began open cars were still painted black, but at midyear Gunmetal Blue and the Phoenix Brown shown here became available as well. Wire wheels and nickle-plated radiator shells were also offered.

Individually none of these changes was particularly dramatic, but together as a group, Ford did a credible job of bringing an aging design in line with contemporary style.

The Model T also gained a functional driver's door on open models. (Previously the door was a dummy.) During the year, base models without electric

starting were dropped. The price of the self-starting touring car opened at an economical $375.

Mechanically, the Model T was little changed. Softer-riding balloon tires became standard during the model year, and brakes were improved to help cope with the extra weight that came along with the restyling. Weight had increased by around 100 pounds (depending on the body style), but the 20-bhp 176.7-cid "flathead" four remained the same, so performance suffered.

Also the same was the two-speed planetary transmission that was shifted by pedals. This system must have been easy for first-time drivers to master, but required holding a pedal to the floor to stay in low gear—tiring when climbing a steep hill. Competitors were offering

conventional three-speed sliding-gear transmissions, better performance, and more contemporary chassis. Still, it's a credit to the soundness of the Model T's basic engineering that a 1908 design was still selling more than 1 million cars a year.

After a sales spurt with the introduction of the '26 cars, production soon resumed its decline. Production for the year came to 1,502,018, which was down more than 300,000 units from the total in 1923.

Even Henry Ford had to admit that a replacement was needed. By time production ended on May 26, 1927, more than 15 million examples of the car that more than any other put America, and arguably the world, on wheels had been produced.

1927 Velie Model 50 Roadster

The name Velie (pronounced vee-lee) might be written off as just another one of the more than 2000 American automobile makes that faded away in the early part of the twentieth century. However, there is more to the Velie story than one would expect. Velie was connected with John Deere farm imple-

ments and built cars, trucks, tractors, fire engines—even airplanes.

Willard Velie was a grandson of John Deere, and was on the Deere and Company Board of Directors. In 1902, Velie founded the Velie Carriage Company. Many carriagemakers turned to making automobiles, and Velie had a

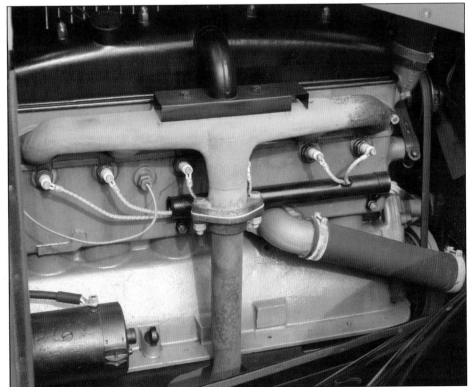

four-cylinder car ready for the 1909 model year. Velie established itself as a medium-price car of good quality.

The company never had a factory team, but some private owners did well racing them. A Velie placed 17th in the inaugural Indianapolis 500 in 1911. Also in 1911, Velie entered the truck market. Although the products of an independent company, Velies were sold through John Deere dealers until 1915. After breaking distribution ties with Deere, Velie added a tractor line, but left the field by 1920.

In 1916, Velie dropped its four to concentrate on making six-cylinder cars. Velie sales peaked at 9000 in 1920, then settled down to a steady 5000. In 1922, the U.S. Navy tested 76 auto engines to identify their best features for adaptation to aircraft motors. Velie's six

was one of only eight that passed the grueling test and was in the company of exalted makes such as Duesenberg, Hispano-Suiza, and Packard—not bad for an obscure midprice car. Velie also proved its durability by driving a car from Los Angeles to the floor of the Grand Canyon and back again with no mechanical trouble. Evidently Velie's "Long Life" slogan was based on fact.

Meanwhile, Willard Velie Jr. became involved in the company. Young Velie was interested in airplanes, and in 1927, Mono Aircraft became a Velie subsidiary. Velie engineers even designed a new five-cylinder radial engine for the plane. Meanwhile, the car line added a straight-eight model for 1928.

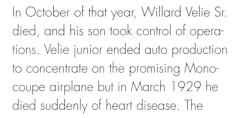

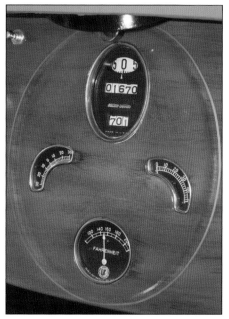

In October of that year, Willard Velie Sr. died, and his son took control of operations. Velie junior ended auto production to concentrate on the promising Monocoupe airplane but in March 1929 he died suddenly of heart disease. The aircraft division was sold to new owners in St. Louis.

The Model 50 shown here was a new design in 1927. The smaller of the two Velie models produced that year, the 50 rode a 112-inch wheelbase and sold for prices starting at a reasonable $1045. The engine was a Velie-built ohv six of 196 cid. It developed 46 bhp and gave a top speed of at least 60 mph. Four-wheel hydraulic bakes were standard.

1929 Cadillac Series 341B Four-Door Town Sedan

Cadillac was due for a "quiet" year in 1929, considering the previous season had seen the arrival of all-new Series 341 cars. They came with attractive styling by Harley Earl, fresh off his success with the 1927 LaSalle; a new 90-bhp 341-cid version of Caddy's established L-head V-8 engine; and a chassis with wheelbase stretched to 140 inches,

a switch to torque-tube drive, and the adoption of 32-inch-diameter tires.

Those core features were indeed carried into 1929, but Cadillac was still able to make some noise in the automotive field—ironically by quieting things down. The marque introduced the "Synchro-Mesh" transmission, which made it easier to shift into second or

third gear without a gratingly audible clash of metal. Other improvements for '29 included internal-expanding brakes at all four wheels (external-contracting bands had been used previously at the rear), double-acting Delco shock absorbers, safety glass, and an adjustable front seat on most models. Fender-top parking lights replaced cowl lamps.

The 1929 Series 341B came in 11 "standard" models with Fisher bodies, plus another dozen "Fleetwood Custom" styles. Among the former was the "Town Sedan" featured here, a close-coupled five-passenger four-door model with a shortened body that made room at the back for a large detachable trunk.

The Cadillac is stunning in its original Pewter Pot, Blue Gray, and Black finish. But it is perhaps the interior details that are most alluring, including the ornate window regulators and door handles, rearview mirror, and dome light; ash receivers set into the door panels; robe rail; and assist straps. The crowning detail, however, is the original broadlace trim that was carefully preserved and returned to the door panels and seatback. When new, the Town Sedan was priced at $3495 to start. Options could add anywhere from $12.50 for the "herald" radiator ornament to $250 for dual sidemount spares and six Buffalo wire wheels. Other accessories include rear and side window shades, aftermarket vases, and a sealskin lap robe.

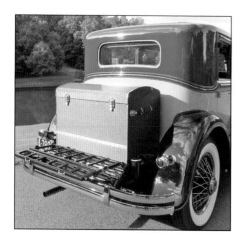

1931 Oakland
Series 301
Sport Coupe

Before Henry Ford brought V-8 ownership to the mass market in 1932, Oakland introduced its own bargain V-8 for 1930. Just as Oakland's companion make, Pontiac, had brought six-cylinder ownership down to a lower price point in 1926, so Oakland hoped to do for the V-8.

Though not exactly popularly priced, the Oakland V-8 could be had for as little as $895, while the cheapest car from V-8 pioneer Cadillac cost $3295. Two design choices helped bring down production costs.

Early V-8 blocks were made up of three castings: one for each bank of cylinders and a third for the crankcase. Oakland (and later Ford) did it in one casting. In fact, General Motors was on a V-8 roll at this time and Oldsmobile's companion make, Viking, also had a "monoblock" V-8 for its short life of 1929-30. However, Viking was more expensive, starting at $1595.

The other cost-cutting measure was the use of a single-plane crankshaft instead of a more expensive two-plane unit. The trade-off was that a one-plane crank caused severe vibrations. Oakland attempted to minimize the problem by mounting the engine on springs and rubber. A vibration damper mounted between the frame and engine was meant to counteract engine movement. These fixes helped, but failed to make the Oakland as smooth as the competition.

One might think that a rough-running engine would shake itself apart, but the Oakland V-8 proved durable in service. The engineers weren't afraid to break with convention and used an unusual horizontal valve layout with the valves mounted high in the block, above the

combustion chambers. This provided some of the performance advantages of overhead valves, but with the ease of manufacture and service of a side-valve engine. An early use of a downdraft carburetor also boosted performance.

The 251-cid V-8 developed 85 bhp, giving Oakland one of the best power-to-weight ratios in its class. Acceleration was lively for the time, and top speed surpassed 70 mph.

Oakland had hoped V-8 power would revive sales, but 21,640 cars were built for 1930 and only 13,408 for 1931. The V-8's introduction coincided with the stock market crash, and divisional companion Pontiac wore the same styling for around $250 less. In the Depression market, Pontiac outsold Oakland by more than 6-to-1 in '31. For 1932, the Oakland V-8 was badged as a Pontiac—and then it was gone.

When new, the 1931 Oakland sport coupe seen here cost $975 and included a rumble seat and golf bag compartment among its standard features.

1933 Dodge HC Station Wagon

In 1933, Dodge was finding its place within Chrysler Corporation. Chrysler purchased Dodge Brothers in 1928 and positioned its cars between DeSoto and Chrysler. By '33, Dodge and DeSoto had swapped places with six-cylinder Dodges wearing prices lower than comparable DeSotos. (Only the soon-to-be-discontinued Dodge Eight cost more).

On the truck front, most of the aging Dodge models designed in the Twenties were replaced by fresh Chrysler-engineered vehicles in '33. Their success moved Dodge up to the number-three sales slot for trucks that it still holds today.

Like many station wagons of the Thirties, our subject here was built on a light-duty truck chassis. In this case,

it's the Dodge HC ½-ton "commercial" chassis with a 111.25-inch wheelbase. The engine was the same 190-cid L-head six used in 1931-32, but with a slight compression boost that raised horsepower to 70 and torque to 130 pound-feet. Top speed was around 40 mph. Factory options on this wagon included its chrome front bumper ($7.50), chrome radiator shell and headlights ($5), and ram radiator cap ($2).

Station wagons of the early Thirties

were usually work vehicles. Hotels often used them to pick up guests and luggage from train stations. Volume was low and most auto companies were happy to let outside firms build wagon bodies on their bare chassis. Because wagons were built in small numbers, it was more economical to pay craftsmen to build wood bodies than to invest in the equipment needed to stamp out metal ones. U.S. Body and Forging Company was Dodge's official wagon supplier in 1933, but other builders could obtain the Dodge chassis. J.T. Cantrell and Company of Huntington, New York, built the wagon seen here. One of this body's interesting details is that only the front doors had roll-up glass windows. All windows aft of the front doors were equipped with snap-in side curtains to offer any protection from inclement weather.

Many "woody" wagon builders were located close to a source of timber, but Long Island-based Cantrell was close to its customers. It catered to wealthy estate dwellers who, like hotels, needed station wagons to pick up guests, luggage, and supplies, and provide transport for hunting and other outdoor activities. Cantrell did a good trade with the East Coast estates, and by the late Thirties had expanded to build factory-cataloged station wagons for Packard and General Motors. The switch to steel-bodied station wagons in the Fifties was a fatal blow to Cantrell's business, and the company ceased operations in 1958.

1937 Chrysler Airflow Four-Door Sedan

When it debuted in 1934, the Airflow was Chrysler's attempt to change the course of automobile design and engineering in the Thirties. Perhaps the most curious part of the Airflow story was that the normally canny Walter Chrysler approved the daring concept without much regard for whether the public would like it. As it played out, the design was successful in nearly every way but sales.

While the Airflow's smooth and rounded aerodynamic shape increased top speed and fuel economy, many car buyers of the day didn't find it as attractive as its boxy competitors. In fact, the styling was polarizing and often resulted in "love it or leave it" reactions.

The body shells were engineered along aircraft principles. This practice resulted in improved strength at less weight.

Another of the Airflow's innovations was moving the engine forward so it was placed over the front axle. The increased room for passengers also allowed the back seat to be located ahead of the rear axle. This change in weight distribution resulted in a better ride—particularly for the rear-seat passengers who no longer sat directly above the pounding rear axle.

On the open road, Airflows cruised comfortably at 65 to 70 mph thanks to Chrysler's early adoption of overdrive. The speedometer featured a built-in tachometer, and a window at the bottom of the dial displayed engine rpms in third gear. When the automatic overdrive engaged, a window at the top of the dial took over. The feature wasn't particularly useful for driving, but Chrysler used it to demonstrate the drop in rpms with overdrive engaged along with the resulting decrease in fuel consumption and engine noise. The Airflow's streamlining also aided quiet cruising.

Power was provided by a 323.5-cid straight eight rated at 130 bhp. An automatic choke aided starting, but if the carburetor flooded, the driver could simply push a small button on the dashboard above the radio to drain the excess gasoline from the carb. The radio was optional, as was the dealer-installed heater.

The Airflow shown here is an end-of-the-road 1937 four-door sedan. It originally priced from $1610, and saw a production run of 4370 units. The only other Airflow model that Chrysler offered that year was the six-passenger coupe. It cost the same but was chosen by only 230 buyers.

The Chrysler Airflow started trends that we take for granted today. The design's unusual appearance and early production problems kept buyers away, but the eventual widespread adoption of some of the Airflow's pioneering principles proved its success in the long run.

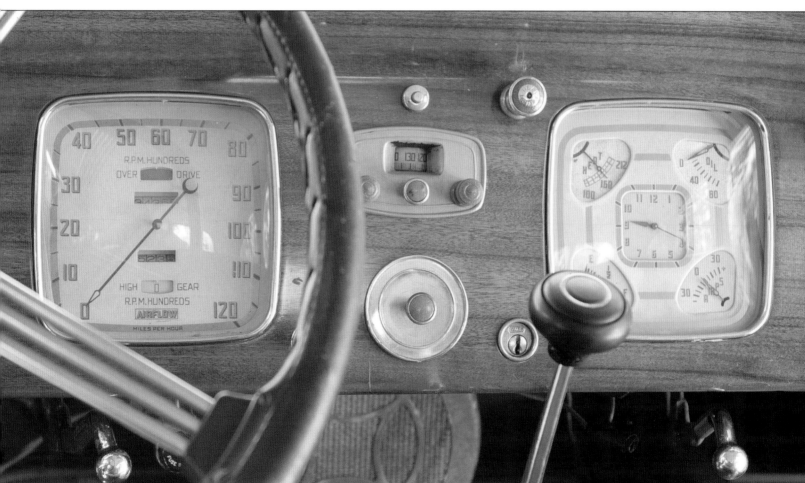

1937 Hudson Country Club Four-Door Touring Sedan

The 1937 Hudsons were much more than met the eye. At a glance, they appeared to be little more than mildly face-lifted 1936 models, but in reality they were far from it. The chassis was beefed up and the wheelbases stretched by two inches. Engines received a two-barrel carburetor, and horsepower was raised across the board. Most importantly, the bodies were all new.

The Hudson lineup was comprised of the Custom Six on a 122-inch wheelbase, along with the DeLuxe Eight and Custom Eight series. The eight-cylinder cars used 122- and 129-inch spans.

The six displaced 212 cubic inches and was good for 101 bhp. The eight was a 254-cube job rated at 122 bhp.

Both engines mated to a three-speed manual transmission with a floor-mount shifter. Hudson's "Electric Hand" vacuum-operated shifter was optional at extra cost. This system allowed preselection of the next gear using a switch and a miniature H gate in a steering-column-mounted pod. The shift would then take place when the clutch pedal was depressed. A new Electric Hand feature for 1937 was the ability to freewheel at speeds below 15 mph.

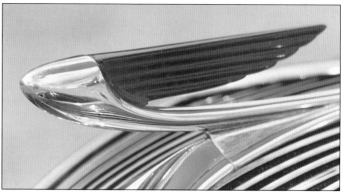

The reworked chassis incorporated the upgrades that were introduced in 1936, including the "Radial Safety Control" front suspension. A hill-holder system was newly available.

Visually, the grille retained the shape used in 1936, but the mesh side sections were replaced with horizontal louvers. Headlamps no longer attached to fender-mounted pedestals but were fixed to the sides of the grille shell.

The bodies were new, and the changes were dramatic. Width was up by about five inches, and overall height was reduced by two. The additional width allowed for three-across seating, front and rear. Company admen said the new interiors possessed "drawing-room beauty." The front doors abandoned the "suicide"-style mounting Hudson adopted for 1932, returning to the more traditional method of locating the hinges at the front pillars.

Most bodies used the 122-inch-wheelbase chassis. The long chassis could be fit with a four-door sedan body, along with a similar Touring sedan type that added an external trunk. The long-wheelbase cars did not seat additional passengers; the added length was used to increase rear-seat legroom. The factory often referred to both of these models as Country Club sedans.

Like most other automakers, Hudson had a challenging 1937. Hudson model-year production fell by more than 22 percent to 20,464, though the company also made 90,253 of its lower-priced Terraplanes.

The featured car is a long-wheelbase Custom Eight Touring sedan. Its base price was $1190. Exact production numbers broken down by body style are not available, but Hudson made a total of 3652 Custom Eights on the long wheelbase for 1937. Regular-wheelbase variants only accounted for another 3274 units, in spite of a much wider array of body styles.

1937 Oldsmobile F-37 Convertible Coupe

Oldsmobile sold a lot of cars in 1937. In fact, with 206,086 produced for the model year, Olds had the best year in its 40-year history. Thanks to robust annual growth, that marked an amazing turnaround from the 20,144 cars that had dribbled out from its assembly lines during the dark days of Depression-wracked 1932.

There were numerous good reasons why Oldsmobile reached a new peak in 1937. For starters, its cars were fully restyled to adorn all-new General Motors-Fisher "B" bodies that newly featured all-steel construction. Furthermore, the division improved both of its available engines and enhanced passenger comfort.

The same seven body styles were available in the six-cylinder F-37 and eight-cylinder L-37 series. Aside from

their engines, they differed in wheelbase and several styling details. Starting prices for the Eights were uniformly $100 more than for the corresponding Sixes, which ranged in price from $685 to $835.

Increases in wheelbase to 117 inches for the F-37 (a gain of two) and to 124 for the L-37 (a gain of three) left room for rear-seat passengers to sit ahead of the axle, a boon to their comfort. The L-head six was bored out by an extra eighth of an inch, which raised displacement to 229.7 cubic inches and boosted horsepower to 95, a gain of five. Meanwhile, the 257.1-cid "flathead" eight was more fundamentally changed and developed 110 bhp.

Where the higher-end cars sported a check pattern on the grille and hood vents, oblong taillight lenses, and decorative bumper plates that called attention their status as eight-cylinder cars, the F-37s went with bold horizontal bars on the grille and hood sides, round taillights in bullet nacelles mounted high on the body, and plainer bumpers. Headlamp

shells differed, too. L-37 interiors also were outfitted with a more elaborate steering wheel and a little more brightwork on the door panels.

All '37 Oldsmobiles featured an X-braced channel-section frame. Suspension was independent and coil-sprung up front; solid-axle supported by semi-elliptic leaf springs in back.

The standard transmission was a three-speed manual, synchronized in the top two gears, and activated by a floor lever. However, a new option—available only for Eights in '37 but later extended to Sixes—was the semiautomatic (and somewhat confusingly named) "Automatic Safety Transmission" with steering-column actuation.

Sixes accounted for 77.5 percent of '37 Oldsmobile output. Of the nearly 160,000 made, 1578 of them were the convertible coupe—now the make's only model with a rumble seat—which headed the line with its $835 starting price. It wasn't a car you would have seen many of in its day and the odds are much longer now.

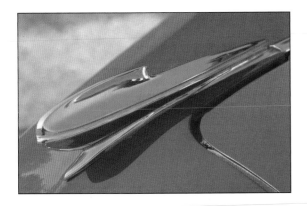

1938 Peugeot 402 B Retractable Hardtop

Chrysler's streamlined 1934 Airflow flopped in America, but it was an inspiration to French automaker Peugeot. With headquarters in Paris and its main plant in Sochaux near the Swiss border, Peugeot is the second-oldest automaker in the world.

In late '35, Peugeot introduced its tribute to Airflow styling with the model 402. The 402's rounded front with waterfall grille was the sincerest form of flattery. Peugeot took streamlining one step further than Chrysler by eliminating running boards and mounting the headlights behind the grille. Peugeot's

streamlining was more than fashion, and the reduced wind resistance improved fuel economy and performance.

Capping the streamlined grille, Peugeot's lion's-head mascot served not only as an ornament, but also as the hood latch. A second stylized lion graced the rear fender skirts.

Most 402s were sedans, but coupes and convertibles were also offered. The most interesting bodystyle was the Éclipse, which was a retractable hardtop. The metal top flipped under the trunklid for open-air motoring, yet offered the security and weather protec-

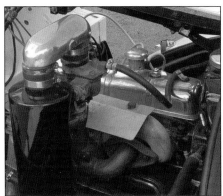

tion of a coupe when raised. Tops on early models were lowered electrically, but starting in '37, a simpler mechanical system that could be operated by one person was used. Peugeot's retractable hardtop was unique in the Thirties. Ford tried the concept again in the Fifties with the Skyliner, but it wasn't until recently that retractable hardtops found commercial success.

Although styling was futuristic, engineering was conventional and lived up to Peugeot's tradition of tough, dependable cars. The Éclipse needed a lengthy 130-inch wheelbase to accommodate a rear deck long enough to swallow the retractable hardtop and to provide room for six passengers on wide bench seats. Independent front suspension contributed to good ride and handling. Power was provided by a 2.1-liter ohv four-cylinder that developed 63 bhp. The standard transmission was a conventional three-speed, but the shifter sprouted through the dashboard instead of the floor.

Fewer than 500 Éclipses were built before production ended in 1940.

1939 Ford
DeLuxe Coupe

Lovely with its Lincoln-Zephyr-inspired styling and lively with its legendary "flathead" V-8 engine, the 1939 Ford coupe entered automotive lore as the basis of many a young driver's hot rod or modified dirt-track racer in which the early stars of professional stock-car racing cut their teeth.

The '39 Fords were significant in that they were the first with the hydraulic brakes that company founder Henry Ford had been stubbornly resisting even as rivals one by one added them. "Big, powerful hydraulic brakes," the '39

sales brochure called them, "precision-built to meet strict Ford standards of safety." (Old Henry was reputed to be quite satisfied with the idea of uninterrupted lengths of steel between his foot and the binders.) The brochure claimed easy pedal action "that will be appreciated by women drivers."

The fluid-pumping master cylinder was bolted to a brake-pedal bracket near the frame's central "X" member. Checking the fluid level required opening a plate in the car's floor. When the "juice" was flowing, it activated 12-inch-diameter drums with twin internal-expanding shoes. Brake-lining area totaled 162 square inches.

Otherwise the chassis carried on little changed with transverse-spring suspensions front and rear. An independent front suspension was still far off in Ford's future, and didn't arrive until the all-new 1949 models.

DeLuxes came only with a 221-cid L-head V-8 officially rated at 85 bhp. Base cars could be equipped with this engine or the two-year-old 136-cube 60-horse "economy" motor. A three-speed transmission with a floor-mounted shifter was standard. (Ford would make the change to a column shift in 1940.) This car is equipped with a rev-lowering Columbia two-speed rear axle, a popular dealer-installed item at the time.

Frontal styling between the two Ford ranges was different. The base cars wore a modified version of the 1938 DeLuxe look, while the very handsome '39 DeLuxes sported a new frontal appearance that was the work of E.T. "Bob" Gregorie with guidance from Edsel Ford. It used a low, wide vee'd radiator grille with vertical bars under a deep, pointed "alligator" hood that did away with side louvers. Headlamps on the upper-level cars in this last year before sealed-beam lighting was adopted were ovoid lenses neatly faired into the forward edge of the fenders.

Ford described the DeLuxe coupe as being a "convenient, modern car . . . desirable for business or professional use." It featured a single bench seat ahead of a large interior cargo space that could be accessed by lifting the seat back. Like all other closed-body '39 Fords, the windshield could—for the last time—be cranked open at the bottom for ventilation.

As a DeLuxe, the $702 coupe enjoyed a number of extras that base cars didn't have. Some of them were twin taillights, wheel trim rings, a "banjo" steering wheel, dual sun visors, a glove-box lock, and clock. Production was 37,326 units.

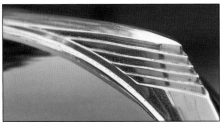

1939 Nash LaFayette Four-Door Sedan

The Thirties proved to be very challenging for the auto industry. Nash weathered the Great Depression about as well as any automaker, but the company did post its first-ever loss in 1933. In an attempt to increase sales and return to profitability, the company introduced the LaFayette as a low-price make in January 1934.

The 1934 LaFayette was not Charles Nash's first experience with a car by that name. Back in 1919, he was behind the LaFayette Motors Corpora-

tion of Indianapolis, a maker of luxury automobiles. By January 1923, the company had relocated to Milwaukee, but the end was near.

In early 1924, LaFayette ceased production and was sold to the Nash-owned Ajax Motors Company. LaFayette's machinery was moved to nearby Racine, Wisconsin, where it was installed in the old Mitchell Motors plant. Nash had recently purchased the factory to produce his new low-price Ajax automobile.

The Ajax lasted about a year before being renamed the Nash Light Six. Less than a decade later, Nash decided to return to the low-price field with a new brand. Interestingly, the firm reprised the name of the failed luxury marque.

LaFayette remained a separate make through 1936. For 1937, the brand became a model name on the entry-level Nash LaFayette 400 Series.

Nash introduced handsome new Ford-like styling for 1939. The company offered 21 models in four series: LaFayette

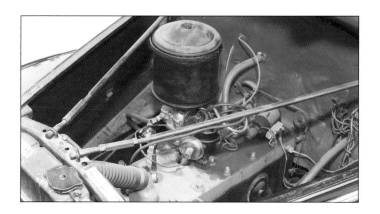

Special, LaFayette Deluxe, Ambassador Six, and Ambassador Eight. LaFayette prices started at $770 for a Special business coupe and went to $950 for a Deluxe convertible coupe. Four-door sedans were available in fastback Slipstream or trunkback designs.

Styling was nearly identical to that of the senior Nash Ambassadors, but the LaFayette's slightly more modest 117-inch wheelbase dictated the use of a shorter hood and running boards. A 234.8-cid L-head six rated at 99 bhp was found under the hood.

New available features included a steering-column-mounted shifter for the three-speed manual transmission and Nash's "Weather Eye" conditioned-air system. Weather Eye improved on the heating and ventilating system Nash introduced for 1938 by offering "automatic" temperature control via an underdash knob.

Weather Eye did not actually cool the air, but the company said incoming fresh air was passed through a filter and moisture shedder to clean it of dust, dirt, insects, snow, and rain. Nash also claimed the system ended the wintertime danger of carbon monoxide buildup in the car's interior.

For 1939, model-year production totaled 49,151, including 37,313 La-Fayettes. This was a dramatic increase over 1938's recession-plagued total of 32,017. Nash last used the LaFayette name in 1940.

1940 Plymouth DeLuxe Convertible

When he launched the Plymouth brand in the middle of 1928, Walter P. Chrysler hoped that it would one day overtake Ford, and 1940 was the year that the marque came closest to achieving that goal. Plymouth's production total of more than 423,000 was within 120,000 units of Ford—and Plymouth might have beaten Ford had not an eight-week strike interrupted production early in the model year. As it was, Plymouth was in third place behind Chevrolet and Ford.

Helping to boost Plymouth's popularity was a longer 117-inch wheelbase that was four and five inches longer than the Chevrolet and Ford competition, respectively. Interior room increased by 10 cubic feet compared to the '39 Plymouths. The engine was shifted forward, and the passenger compartment was located well ahead of the rear axle. This provided good balance for a better ride and improved handling.

Plymouth's 201.3-cid "flathead" six developed 84 bhp—within one horsepower of the larger-displacement Chevy six and Ford V-8. The economical Plymouth six could cruise at 60 mph but those seeking more from it could order a high-compression head that upped horsepower to 87 on the required premium-grade fuel. Additionally, a low-compression 65-bhp "economy" engine was available.

Plymouth had all-new bodies for 1940. Appearance changes were evolutionary, and although styling was similar to that of the previous year, the Mayflower hood ornament was the only body part that carried over. And, like other cars from Detroit, there were new round sealed-beam headlamps up front.

The convertible was perhaps the most changed body style. The day of the drafty rumble seat was over; Plymouth wisely replaced it with folding seats within the passenger compartment. Now up to four passengers could be protected from the weather under the canvas top. Plymouth was the first to offer a power-operated convertible top in 1939, and the vacuum-assisted top returned for 1940.

The base price of this convertible was $950, which didn't include the optional fog lights, spotlight, and heater. Leather

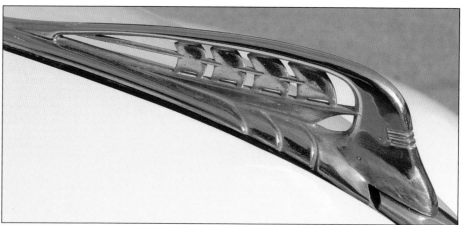

upholstery was standard. Running boards were a popular delete option. However, the convertible had a special reinforced frame that resulted in a higher floor. For this reason, Plymouth recommended that convertible buyers not delete running boards.

Plymouth sold 6986 convertibles in what was largely a good year for the

brand. But unfortunately, 1940 was also the year Walter P. Chrysler died.

Well engineered and nicely styled, the 1940 Plymouth was a solid entry among the "low-priced three" that gave Ford a run for its money and was the basis for cars that served Chrysler Corporation well until the first all-new postwar models arrived in 1949.

1941 Buick Special Sedanet

Buick's powerful and stylish 1941 models were a hit, with a prewar record 377,428 built. The entry-level Special led the charge with 242,089 of that total. Part of the Special's appeal was all-new styling and a new body style dubbed the "sedanet" that had the look of a rakish fastback coupe but afforded sedanlike room for six passengers.

Styling was evolutionary. Headlights were moved out to the edges of the fenders, which themselves were now more integrated with the hood. A broader grille accentuated the car's width, and there were revised "ports" on the front fenders.

The hood was now a single panel which helped improve access to the engine. Interestingly, the hood could be opened from either side of the car by pulling out the "Louvre-Lock," a hood

latch that blended in nicely with the side trim. By pulling both latches, it was possible to remove the hood entirely.

At the start of production, Specials were offered in two-door "sedanet" and four-door models, along with a wood-bodied Estate Wagon. Midyear, Buick added a Special subseries that shared notchback "A" bodies with Chevrolet. This new Special line included a business coupe, sport coupe, four-door sedan, and convertible on a 118-inch

wheelbase that was three inches shorter than the span used on the original Specials.

Somewhat confusingly, the late arrivals were designated "Series 40-A" models while the original fastback Specials became "Series 40-B" models. The "A" and "B" in each name was a reference to the body family.

Supers were fitted with Buick's 248-cubic-inch "Fireball" straight eight-cylinder engine. There was a horse-

power boost from the 1940 rating of 107 to 115, thanks to new "Turbolator" high-compression pistons.

Buick's other innovation for 1941 was "Compound Carburation." Essentially it was two two-barrel carburetors working in series. The primary carb handled part-load driving, while the secondary unit engaged during full-throttle acceleration. This setup allowed the 248-cubic-inch Fireball Eight to pick up an additional ten horsepower for a total of 125.

Special buyers could dress up their new cars with an SE (for Super-Equipped) trim option which included the interior appointments from Buick's more expensive Super model along with the dual-carb engine. There was also an optional Super Sonomatic five-band radio that provided short-wave reception to help owners keep up with fast-changing world news.

The '41 Special sedanet on these pages was one of just 9614 ordered with the "Super-Equipped" package. As such, it sold for a reasonable $1063.

1941 Packard One Sixty Deluxe Convertible Coupe

Packard's policy of gradual styling changes helped it to maintain a gold standard of resale value and allowed owners to keep their cars longer without looking dated. This linear styling policy served Packard well until the Forties. By then, though, American car design was changing at an incredible rate. Packard's unhurried design evolution couldn't keep up with the pace, and by '41, its cars looked old-fashioned.

But Packard wasn't out. Late in the 1941 model year, Packard brought out its highly acclaimed Clipper, which was

lower, wider, and more modern than the competition. Packard styling was once again esteemed. The company was in the process of replacing its old-style bodies with Clipper styling when World War II broke out. (The obsolete design did have an unexpected admirer in Soviet Premier Joseph Stalin. Russia's ZIS 110, made from 1946 to 1959, copied 1941-42 Packard styling.)

Although not well received in '41, to modern eyes, the Packard One Sixty Deluxe convertible coupe shown here looks like a classic example of a prewar convertible. Styling was subtly modern-

ized for 1941, with the headlamps integrated into the front fenders and capped with prominent chrome spears holding the parking lights at their tips.

Most makes had phased out side-mount spares by '41, but the upright styling of the One Sixty carries them well. Running boards were also on the way out—Packard had moved them to the options list.

Although One Sixtys were senior-model Packards, they shared body panels and a 127-inch wheelbase with the medium-price One Twenty (though there were some longer-wheelbase One Sixty sedans). They did have more upscale trim, and this was most evident in the interior. The convertible offered a choice of cloth and leather or full leather—as on this car. As a Deluxe model, the featured car has inlaid wood window trim. By the Forties, American luxury cars had replaced real wood with plastic moldings or woodgrain painted on metal, but the wood window trim on this car is as fine as in any custom body from Twenties or Thirties.

Another interesting trim detail in the interior involved the control knobs on either side of the steering column. To operate these controls, the driver grabbed rectangular handles that were shaped, and colored, like a Kit-Kat candy bar.

What really set the senior Packards apart from the One Twenty was their big 356-cid straight eight. New for 1940, this heavy engine was incredibly smooth and quiet. It had a sturdy 105-pound crankshaft running in nine main bearings, and was the first Packard with hydraulic valve lifters. The motor put out 160 bhp (10 more than Cadillac's V-8) and could push the two-ton convertible past 100 mph.

Packard built at least 128 One Sixty Deluxe convertible coupes for '41; only 19 are known to have survived. The Deluxe drop top priced from $2112, while a base model listed from $1937.

1941 Willys 441 Station Wagon

In the "baby boom" Fifties, Americans came to embrace the station wagon in a big way. It was just the right kind of motor vehicle for families expanding both in size and in number. But it was a friendship that took time to grow.

Prior to World War II, the station wagon was a little harder to like. Almost uniformly constructed with wood bodies, early wagons needed to be serviced as much as they served. Still, their ranks grew steadily throughout the Thirties as,

one by one, automakers began adding them to their factory-cataloged rosters.

Even the smallest of manufacturers eventually felt compelled to enter the field. Among them was Willys-Overland of Toledo, Ohio. In 1940, Willys

added an $830 wagon to its 440 DeLuxe line with a U.S. Body and Forging Company body manufactured in Frankfort, Indiana.

The following year, the wagon came back bigger and better than before because the compact four-cylinder Willys was bigger and better than ever. For starters, wheelbase grew to 104 inches, a gain of two inches. Frontal styling was revised with cleaner hood decoration and a low, uninterrupted vertical-bar grille, a change from 1940's divided unit. Teardrop-shaped bezels held new sealed-beam headlights (Willys switched to the improved lights a year after most other American makes) and integrated the parking lights.

Horsepower from the 134.2-cid L-head engine was nudged up to 63 (from 61) and a hypoid rear axle was adopted.

Willys began marketing its Series 441 as the Americar. Body-style offerings remained the same—business coupe, four-door sedan, and wagon—but a new Plainsman level with overdrive and a finned high-compression head was added above the continued Speedway and DeLuxe lines.

The six-passenger station wagon continued to be offered only at the DeLuxe level. Willys promoted it as "the answer to the need for a fine low cost estate wagon," and added, "This fine car is beautifully appointed, has large roomy interiors, a powerful thrifty engine, speed, power, easy handling, easy riding and dependability." The price was boosted to $916 for '41.

A synchronized three-speed transmission, with the column shifter that was made standard throughout the Willys line

for '41, was hooked to the undersquare four. Accessories included a heater, wheel trim rings, and whitewall tires.

The car sat on an "X"-braced frame that was widened and strengthened for 1941. Leaf springs were used at all four corners, with a semifloating axle in back paired with a reverse-Elliott-type I-beam axle in the front.

The Willys "woody" wagon made its final appearance in 1942, when it sold for $978 to start. Total production for all 1941 and 1942 Americar models was only 28,935 before Willys-Overland shifted entirely to war production.

Buoyed by the battlefield success of the little four-wheel-drive "jeep" that it built by the hundreds of thousands during the war, Willys would use it to inspire a new kind of station wagon—one with an easy-to-care-for steel body—in 1946. For the new postwar baby-boom families, the modern station wagon couldn't have come along at a better moment.

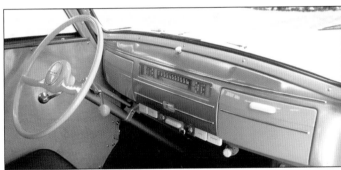

1942 Dodge DeLuxe Business Coupe

Dependability had been the watchword at Dodge since Horace and John Dodge built their first car in 1914. With war clouds gathering as the 1942 line was introduced in late 1941, dependability became even more important.

Many car buyers had a sinking feeling that the '42 model they were buying might have to serve through the duration of a conflict.

To introduce its 1942 cars, Dodge made a promotional film with Jimmie

Lynch of Jimmie Lynch's Death Dodgers, an auto-daredevil show that—perhaps appropriately—used Dodges. Lynch drove the new Dodge over railroad ties, sent it airborne off ramps, and finished with his "roll of death." The Dodge was

battered, but still drivable. This was more than hype. Dodges of that era weren't excitement machines, but they were solid and dependable.

Among the improvements for '42 was a bigger L-head six-cylinder engine. Enlarged from 218 to 230 cid, its horsepower rating rose from 87 to 105. Fuel economy became a concern with the imposition of wartime gas rationing, but Dodge held up its end here. In spite of its bigger engine, Dodge was able to boast that in a nationwide test, its '42 model averaged 21.64 mpg.

Optional Fluid Drive came to Dodge in 1941 and was still heavily promoted in '42. Fluid Drive was basically a semi-automatic transmission that replaced the flywheel with a fluid coupling. Slippage in the coupling allowed the car to come to a complete stop while in gear without releasing the clutch. Fluid Drive also reduced the need to downshift from high in the three-speed gearbox. One could even start from a dead stop in high, although acceleration off the line was

leisurely. No other car in Dodge's price range offered the Fluid Drive's convenience of reduced shifting and clutching.

Even though our featured DeLuxe business coupe was the least expensive '42 Dodge at $895 to start, this example was built with the pricey Fluid Drive option. Of the 68,522 Dodges built for

the war-shortened 1942 model year, 5257 were three-passenger business coupes, a style not available in the costlier Custom series. With its glistening chrome, this coupe was built before mid-December '41—when government "blackout" rules required that bright trim be eliminated or painted over.

1942 Pontiac Streamliner Chieftain Six Sedan Coupe

General Motors was on a fastback kick when this 1942 Pontiac Streamliner sedan coupe was built. Introduced in 1941 as the corporate B-body design, the fastbacks were available in two- and four-door styles. With the addition of a two-door fastback to the lineup of smaller "A" bodies for '42, all five GM car divisions offered the sleek look.

Fastbacks were the final evolution of the Thirties streamlining trend. Popular in the Forties, they faded by the early

Fifties as cars became more squared off and the hardtop replaced the fastback as the "sporty" body style.

Pontiac grouped its 1942 B-body fastbacks in the Streamliner series, which offered a choice of standard or more deluxe Chieftain trim, all built on a 122-inch wheelbase. (A-body Pontiacs on a 119-inch wheelbase were dubbed Torpedoes.) Streamliners could be had as a four-door sedan, sedan coupe—Pontiac's particular term for the two-door

fastback—or wood-bodied four-door station wagon.

The 1942 Pontiac's wind-cheating look was enhanced with new front fenders. The fenderline extended well into the door panel and gave the heightened impression of motion.

All Pontiacs had a choice of inline six- or eight-cylinder engines. The eight was a $25 upgrade regardless of model. Most '42 Torpedo customers ordered a six, while Streamliner buyers preferred the eight by a margin of more than two-to-one. Thus, our featured car with the 239-cid 90-bhp six is quite rare: Of the 83,555 Pontiacs built for the model year, just 2458 were six-cylinder Streamliner Chieftains. Compared to the eight, the six was only 10 cid smaller with 13 less horsepower. The six didn't

sacrifice much in terms of power, and its slightly better fuel economy must have been appreciated during World War II-era gas rationing.

Pontiac engines of this era were simple L-heads that were easy to build and maintain. They were also reliable and served well during the war years.

In fact, the last American car to roll off an assembly line as the U.S. entered the conflict was a Pontiac. But it wasn't our photo feature car, which was built in November 1941—well before the War Production Board's February 10, 1942, deadline to end civilian production.

Remarkably, this Pontiac's interior is still original, but the owner has protected the wool upholstery with NOS seat covers of the kind commonly installed by new-car buyers in 1942.

1947 Triumph 1800 Roadster

Triumph might have died in 1939 if it hadn't been for Sir John Black's bad temper and Jaguar envy. Sir John was the unpredictable, but effective, manager of Standard Motor Company, Ltd. He was famous for wild mood swings.

Standard supplied engines for early Jaguars and at one time Sir John wanted absorb the burgeoning Jaguar into Standard. William Lyons of Jaguar refused.

Sir John decided Standard wouldn't build Jaguar sixes after World War II but would sell Jaguar the tooling. Lyons knew to jump on the deal before Sir

John changed his mind—which he did. Black was used to getting his way and took offense. He decided to beat Jaguar at its own game.

Before the war, Triumph made a name, but not much money, building upper-medium-priced cars with a sporting reputation and some success in rallies. With the Triumph name and Standard's resources, Black planned to put Jaguar out of business. Unfortunately by VE Day there wasn't much left of Triumph other than the name. What hadn't been sold off had been bombed by the Germans.

Jaguar unwittingly helped with the engine. Although Standard had stopped building Jaguar sixes, it still built Jaguar's 1800cc four. This engine started out as a Standard side-valve, but in the mid Thirties, Jaguar added a new cylinder head with overhead valves for increased power. The 63-bhp unit was the only suitable engine Standard had for its new sporting Triumphs. The four-cylinder Jaguar and Triumph also shared the same four-speed transmission, although Jaguar used a floor shift while Triumph's shift was on the column. The Triumph

Roadster was not a sports car, but it was sporting. Top speed was 77 mph, and 0-60 took 25.2 seconds. *Motor* described the Roadster as having "a distinctly better than average all-round performance." The '47 Volkswagen, for example, never made it to 60 but topped out at 57.3 mph in *Motor* tests.

The chassis used a Standard independent front suspension with a transverse leaf spring. Sheet steel was severely rationed in postwar England, so tubular steel was used for the frame. The price for a '47 Roadster was a rather steep £775; the cheapest Jaguar sedan with same engine cost £676.

Although the body was new, it had a prewar flavor with its classic chrome radiator and pontoon fenders. Open-air rumble seats faded away in the late Thirties, but Triumph had the distinction of building the last rumble seat. The last was perhaps the best because opening the seat raised a second windshield

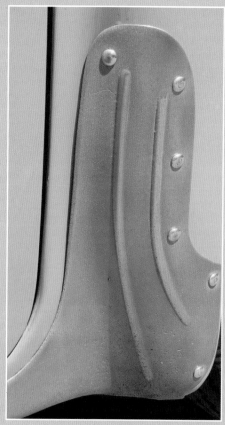

that offered some wind protection. The roadster sat five, two in the rumble seat and three crammed in leather-and-wood luxury on the front bench seat. The Roadster was a modest success with 4500 built between 1946 and 1949. Triumph didn't put Jaguar out of business, but its name would supplant Standard.

1948 Ford Sedan Coupe

The Forties brought great challenges to the American automobile industry, and the Ford Motor Company faced not only external turmoil but internal chaos as well. After Edsel Ford died in May 1943, the company was increasingly controlled by the ruthless Harry Bennett, the chief aide and hatchet man to Henry Ford during the Thirties and Forties.

That August, young Henry Ford II, Edsel's oldest son, was released from duty in the U.S. Navy to help his grandfather run the company, particularly to make sure the firm was able to deliver on its critical wartime military contracts. By December 1943, young "HFII" was named an executive vice president of Ford, but the elder Ford and Bennett didn't appreciate having the 26-year-old scion around.

Throughout 1944 and into the next year, Henry Ford's wife, Clara, and Edsel's widow, Eleanor, put great pressure on the old man to hand over control of the company to his grandson. He finally gave in, and Henry II was named company president on September 21, 1945. One of the first things he did was to fire Harry Bennett.

Just months before, on July 3, Ford became the first company to resume postwar passenger-car production in the U.S. Not

surprisingly, the 1946 Ford was a mildly warmed-over 1942 model. Still, this "new" car was very similar in concept to the pattern set with the 1932 model: beam front axle, transverse leaf springs, torque-tube drive, and Ol' Henry's "flat-head" V-8.

The L-head V-8 was revised with several internal improvements and an increase in displacement to match the Mercury at 239.4 cid. For the first time, the Ford and Mercury V-8s were rated the same—100 bhp. The 226-cid 90-horsepower six-cylinder engine that had debuted in 1941 was back too.

Exterior sheetmetal was little changed from 1942, but a fresh grille made up of horizontal bars presented a new face to the world. Interior trim was upgraded with brighter colors and better materials.

Of course, buyers appreciated the improvements, but in those early postwar days, the seller's market meant that the buying public was pretty much happy with whatever it could get.

The elder Henry Ford died on April 7, 1947. About that time, the company replaced the carried-over 1946-style models with the cars many consider to be the "real" '47s.

The minor update introduced some appearance and feature changes, a few of which were obviously intended to keep production costs under control. In the August 1947 issue of *Mechanix Illustrated*, outspoken car tester Tom Mc-Cahill groused that Ford had taken cost out of the 1947 models by eliminating certain features. The springtime '47s continued into the following year unchanged until the all-new 1949s arrived at dealers in June 1948.

Ford dubbed its five-passenger club coupe a "Sedan Coupe." The 1948 Super DeLuxe version seen here is equipped with a Columbia two-speed rear axle and several period accessories including road lamps, exterior mirrors, and bumper end guards.

1949 Anglia Two-Door Sedan

Ford's history in Great Britain dates to the earliest days of the company when in 1903 a small batch of cars was imported from America. By 1911, Ford's British operations were assembling the Model T locally, but the first cars specifically designed for the English market did not arrive until the Thirties.

After World War II, Ford of Britain was able to restart civilian production by June 1945. Within a few years, some dealers in the United States were peddling a selection of British-built Ford products including Anglia and Prefect sedans and Thames light-duty trucks.

The Anglia was based on the 7Y Eight model that went on sale in September 1937. The four-passenger car

was 148.5 inches long with a 90-inch wheelbase. Sold only as a two-door saloon (a sedan to Americans), the 7Y had fender-mounted headlamps, a center-hinged hood, and a rear-mounted spare tire. The engine was a

933cc/56.9-cid L-head four rated at 23.4 bhp. The chassis and driveline followed typical Ford design practices with transverse-leaf springs front and rear, a three-speed manual transmission, torque-tube drive, and mechanical brakes.

In 1940, the car was renamed Anglia. At the same time, it received a nearly upright grille, a longer hood, and a built-in trunk. After the war, the car benefited from an upgraded electrical system, improved rust resistance, and larger brakes. A slightly revised grille appeared for 1948.

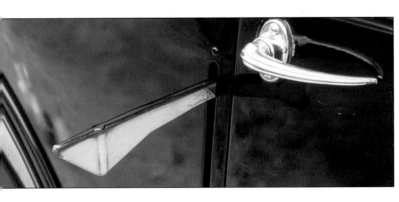

The Anglia received another facelift for 1949. The "new" look was heavily based on the front sheetmetal from the original 7Y Eight, but a body-color divider followed the centerline of the car and split the grille into two sections. Each narrow opening was filled with an insert. The minor restyling proved to be attractive and the car carried on virtually unchanged until a modern new Anglia appeared in fall 1953.

At that point, the old Anglia was rechristened the Popular and remained in production for six more years. The low-price Popular was powered by an 1172cc/71.6-cid four cylinder, which was a 30.1-bhp engine that had previously been fitted to the slightly larger Prefect sedan and Anglias destined for export markets.

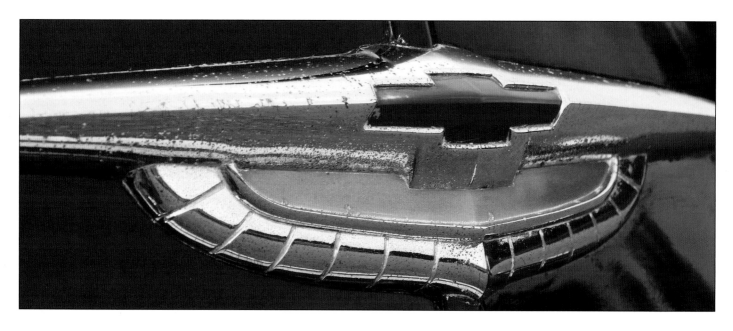

1950 Chevrolet Special Styleline Two-Door Sedan

The 1949 Chevrolets were a tough act to follow, even if the next act was the 1950 Chevrolet. After all, the '49s were the division's first all-new cars after World War II. But rather than be a "me-too" model year—which would have been expected—1950 was when Chevy rolled out its first two-door hardtop model and the first automatic transmission available in the low-price field. Plus, there were other subtle changes found throughout the line.

The featured machine is a relatively untouched 1950 Special Styleline two-door sedan. The HJ-series Special was

the base series, lacking the bright-metal front and rear window frames and some of the bodyside trim found on the HK DeLuxe. As a Styleline, it was one of four notchback body styles in the lineup. (There were two fastback Fleetline sedans available too.)

A bow-shaped upper grille with blue Chevrolet lettering was retained from 1949. But directly above and below this bow were the detail changes that distinguished the face of the '50s.

A larger emblem, now filled with gold paint, adorned the hood. The lower grille featured individual triple-grooved bars under each parking light rather than the seven vertical bars of 1949. Larger front and rear bumper guards

were now standard on all Chevys. The original invoice for this car lists accessory fender guards, which attached to the ends of the bumpers and wrapped around the fenders to provide additional protection to the sheetmetal.

Other exterior changes for '50 were hubcaps with a gold paint fill in place of red and an elaborate combined trunk handle and chrome decklid ornament that mimicked the shape of the hood emblem. Specials ordinarily came with black rubber gravel guards on the rear fenders, but this car wears accessory stainless steel guards that were standard on DeLuxes.

All Specials had striped gray cloth upholstery and a harmonizing gray

three-spoke steering wheel. Comforts and conveniences were few. Our feature car was delivered with an optional heater and defroster and a directional-signal unit is attached to the left side of the steering column. Back-up lights are another extra-cost add-on.

Offered only with a three-speed synchromesh transmission, Specials were powered by an ohv 216.5-cid inline six-cylinder engine with a cast-iron block and single-barrel carburetor good for 92 horsepower.

The Styleline sedans were the most popular of Chevrolet's Special series in 1950, with 89,897 of the two-door model 1502s produced at a base price of $1403.

1950 DeSoto Custom Station Wagon

The wood-bodied station wagon was in its twilight years by 1950. It had progressed from commercial depot hack in the Teens and Twenties to something of a status symbol in the Thirties and Forties. Station wagons were just

the thing for hunting trips or carrying riding tack to and from the stables. In the 1939 movie *Dark Victory*, Bette Davis's socialite-horsewoman character describes herself as part of the "station wagon crowd."

By then wagons were well styled and crafted. The fine wood suggested yachts and required almost as much maintenance. Proper care meant yearly varnishing but even then the wood could rot, and sections needed to be

replaced. Changes in temperature caused wood to expand or contract. Screws and bolts had to periodically be tightened to avoid squeaks and rattles.

Meanwhile, families of more average means noticed that wagons would be good to carry a growing family and its gear. However, the station wagon was often the most expensive bodystyle in a make's lineup, and nobody wanted to add varnishing the family car to the list of household chores. The steel-bodied

station wagon changed that. A new kind of station wagon crowd was more likely to be seen at Scout jamborees or PTA meetings than at horse shows.

Willys and Crosley built the first steel station wagons, but the Crosley was a tiny subcompact and the Willys was more of a sport-utility vehicle. The first mainstream full-size steel wagon was the 1949 Plymouth Suburban. By 1953, Buick was building the last American wagon with structural-wood construction. However, many people liked the "woody" look and woodgrain appliqués were applied to steel wagons to evoke a bygone era.

The 1950 DeSoto Custom featured here was among the last DeSoto wagons with real wood. DeSoto followed Plymouth's lead and replaced its woody with a steel-bodied wagon late in the 1950 model year. Only 600 wood

wagons were built in 1950. Perhaps only two or three restored examples remain.

The upright styling beloved by Chrysler Corporation President K. T. Keller worked well on the station wagon. For 1950, there was a new variation of the brand's toothy grille, and a hood ornament that featured the helmeted head of Hernando de Soto with a plastic face that glowed when the headlights were lit. Underhood was a 236.6-cid six that developed 112 bhp. The engine was more impressive than its specifications. It included a high-compression head, well-engineered ignition system, and low-friction Superfinish internal parts to reduce wear. A three-speed manual transmission was standard on base DeLuxe models, while Customs had a semiautomatic transmission dubbed "Tip-Toe Hydraulic Shift with gyrol Fluid Drive."

1951 Chrysler Windsor Highlander Newport Hardtop Coupe

Nineteen fifty-one was the year of the "hemi" at Chrysler. Saratogas, New Yorkers, and Imperials all got the brand-new 331-cid "FirePower" ohv V-8, a sensation with its efficient hemispherical combustion chambers and 180 bhp.

That certainly left the Windsor series, with its staid flathead six, in the shade.

But the Windsor—now Chrysler's entry-level series with the demise of the Royal—had sufficient charms of its own. Not the least of them was its availability

as a stylish Newport two-door hardtop or the chance to order it with the Highlander interior.

The pillarless hardtop body was in its second year at Chrysler, and the shape of the roof was unchanged from 1950.

As was common at the time, Chrysler gave a distinct name to its hardtops: Regardless of series, they were Newports. In '51, the Windsor was offered in base and Deluxe trim, but only the Windsor Deluxe could be a Newport, which started at $2953. The Highlander interior option, which featured colorful plaid cloth on the seat cushions, back rests, and door panels, had been available on certain New Yorker and Windsor models since 1940.

Chrysler combined production figures for its 1951 and '52 cars so breakdowns by model year are not available. It's estimated that about 6400 of the 10,200 Windsor Deluxe hardtops made in the period were '51s.

The 1951 Chryslers were extensively facelifted versions of the first all-new postwar designs the division created for 1949. Central to the new look were a two-bar grille and a laid-back, more streamlined hood than that found on the 1949-50 cars.

Chassis were carried over, too. In the case of the Windsor, that was a 125.5-inch wheelbase (139.5 for eight-passenger models) with independent coil-spring suspension in front and Hotchkiss-type drive with semielliptic leaf springs in back.

As noted, only the Windsor retained its previous engine. The 250.6-cid L-head six generated 116 bhp. It was hooked to a three-speed manual transmission with the availability of Chrysler's famous Fluid Drive system, which the featured car has.

1951 Jowett Jupiter Convertible

Jowett was an unorthodox make even by British standards. From 1910 through 1936, Jowetts were powered by horizontally opposed two-cylinder engines. A four introduced in '36 continued the "boxer" layout in which the two banks of cylinders faced each other with the crankshaft in the middle. Then, too,

Jowett was located off the beaten path in the Yorkshire village of Idle. (Management must have gotten tired of "Idle factory" jokes.)

In 1947, Jowett introduced its technologically advanced Javelin sedan. The unitary body was aerodynamic for the time. Springing at both ends was

by torsion bars with independent front suspension. Jowett stuck with the horizontal engine design, the like of which is only used by Subaru and Porsche today. The ohv four displaced just 1.5 liters (90 cid) and developed 50 bhp. Thanks to low weight of not much more than a ton, the Javelin had good performance for a small sedan of its time, and won its class in the 1949 Monte Carlo Rally.

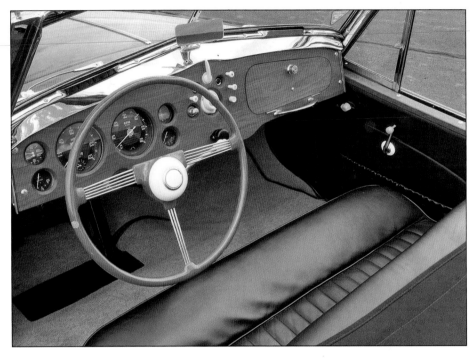

Encouraged by its Monte Carlo victory, Jowett decided to build a sports car using Javelin components for 1950, the Jupiter. Its backbone was a tubular chrome-moly-steel chassis. Torsion-bar suspension was retained, but Jupiter gained rack-and-pinion steering. As in the Javelin, the lightweight aluminum engine sat ahead of the front axle line with the radiator mounted behind the engine. Horsepower was increased to 60. Unusual for a sports car, the four-speed transmission retained the Javelin's column-mounted shifter.

The chassis was clothed in an aluminum convertible body with roll-up windows. The interior was well finished and roomy for a sports car—Jowett claimed three-passenger capacity. In spite of the amenities, the Jupiter weighed only 1500 pounds. Performance was good with 0-60 mph in 15 seconds, and a top speed of around 90. Performance and handling helped Jupiter win in its class at Le Mans from 1950 through 1952.

Jowett hoped Jupiter would do well on the American market, but weak crankshafts and a few other problems gave the car a reputation for unreliability. The problems were ironed out but the damage was done. Not helping was a Tom McCahill review in *Mechanix Illustrated* that said the Jupiter "dives into corners like a porpoise with heartburn and the steering is like winding an eight-day clock with a broken mainspring." *Road & Track*, which later reviewed the Jupiter, liked its handling and speculated that there might have been something wrong with McCahill's car.

Approximately 900 Jupiters had been built by the time Jowett production ended in 1954.

1952 Buick Special DeLuxe Four-Door Sedan

The featured car is an example of the second-most-popular Buick of '52. Orders for 63,346 Special DeLuxe four-doors were placed that model year; only the Super four-door sedan moved more metal from Buick showrooms.

The well-rounded Special lineup included two- and four-door sedans, a club coupe, a convertible, and a Riviera two-door hardtop, with starting prices that ran from $2115 to $2634. All but the coupe came with DeLuxe equip-

ment, which consisted of an undivided windshield, bright rocker-panel trim, and bolted-on chrome tailfins. There was a nicer grade of cloth on the interior, too.

There was a "standard" four-door sedan that lacked these items. It sold for $46 less than the $2255 that Buick charged for the DeLuxe four-door, but it was discontinued early in the year with just 137 made. (A base two-door sedan and business coupe shown in sales literature apparently weren't built.)

Specials were mounted on a 121.5-inch wheelbase, as they had been since 1950. Styling was a virtual repeat of 1951, but it remained distinctively Buick's own: sweepspears, portholes, bullet-in-circle hood ornaments, and big chrome "buck-tooth" grilles were recognizable Flint hallmarks. Sheetmetal went untouched, but there were slightly modified front bumper guards, a new wheel-cover design, a simplified canti-lever bodyside "sweepspear," and the rear-fender fins that were applied to all models but the base-trim Specials.

Also untouched was Buick's aging but proven powerplant, a 263.3-cid ohv straight eight. With the standard three-speed synchromesh transmission, it soldiered on at 120 bhp at 3600 rpm.

However, when hooked to the $193 Dynaflow torque-converter automatic transmission output rose to 128 horsepower, thanks to a bump in compression from 6.6:1 to 7.2:1.

Dynaflow Drive (some called it "Dyna-Slush") had been introduced as a standard Roadmaster item in late 1947. It soon became a popular option on other Buick models. Its torque convertor

system depended on induced rotation of a drive turbine through an oil bath by a facing crankshaft-driven turbine. Dynaflow was very smooth in operation, but not exciting in performance.

Other extra-cost items on the featured car include wheel covers, whitewall tires, back-up lamps, a radio, and two-tone paint.

For the year, Buick was a solid fourth in the industry sales race, but shortages caused by a nationwide steel strike and defense requirements for the war in Korea limited output. Buick production for 1952 was 301,702 units, a dramatic reduction from the more than 667,000 cars built in 1950.

1952 Healey Tickford Saloon

Donald Healey is famous for the Austin-Healey, but he had an active life long before he teamed up with Austin. Healey flew for the Royal Flying Corps during World War I. Between the wars he was a successful rally driver and won the 1931 Monte Carlo Rallye. Later he was director of experimental design at Triumph. During World War II he worked on armored-car design.

After the war, Donald Healey set up a company to produce his vision of a grand touring machine. Production started in fall 1946. The new Healey featured independent front suspension and a robust frame for good handling. For power, Healey bought 2.4-liter four-

cylinder engines made by Riley, another English automaker. With advanced features such as hemispherical combustion chambers and dual camshafts mounted high in the block, 104 bhp was developed. Thanks to sound engineering and development of the basic design since

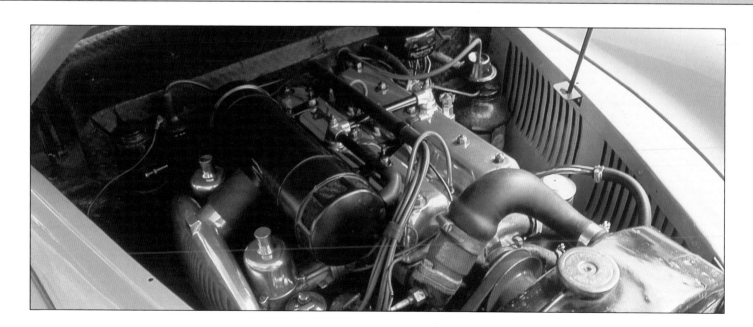

1926, the Riley engine proved to be tough and reliable.

Several small coachbuilders supplied bodies. Four-seat convertibles and coupes were the most popular, and this coupe has bodywork by Tickford. A shortened two-seat Silverstone sports car was also offered. Although the coupes had two doors and only a small back seat, Healey called them saloons—British for sedan.

Healey was quick to enter his cars in competition, and strong showings in rallies generated good publicity. In 1947, a production car was sent to Belgium for speed runs and was timed at 110.8 mph. For a time, Healey was able to advertise his car as "The fastest production car in the world."

The Healey chassis received several refinements during production. The car

also gained weight but was still good for more than 100 mph. With good handling and a willing engine, Healeys were a joy to drive. They were also expensive. An early convertible cost $7500 in the U.S. when a 1947 Ford sold for $1154.

Healey also built the Nash-Healey using Nash engines in a Healey chassis. The Nash-Healey was also expensive and Donald set about designing a more affordable car using Austin components. The Austin-Healey was such a hit at the Earls Court Motor Show that Austin

offered to take over production, and work on the new car soon dominated Healey's firm.

Although the Healey was profitable, its Riley engine was set to go out of production. Healey sales ended in '54 after about 700 cars had been built.

1952 Packard Pan American Convertible

As noted historian George Hamlin recounted in a profile of Packard Pan American designer Richard Arbib, the Pan American was one of several "sports car" ideas that the styling consultant doodled up for the Henney Body Company of Freeport, Illinois, long a supplier of Packard-based hearses, ambulances, and other professional cars.

A successful industrial designer since the late Thirties, Arbib had also worked

for General Motors and, after the war, the Harley Earl Corporation. When a falling out with Earl prompted him to go freelance in 1949, Arbib contacted a previous employer, industrialist Charles Russell Feldmann. As it happened, Feldmann had just purchased Henney (for a second time) and needed help with redesigning its professional coachwork to match Packard's new 1951 "high pockets" styling. Arbib duly signed on as a Henney consultant and de facto one-man styling staff.

Feldmann wanted to expand Henney's business, in part by "doing something

in the sports car area," as the designer later recalled. Encouraged to let his imagination roam with hopes of winning more Packard contracts, Arbib drew up a two-seat sports convertible based on John Reinhart's 1951 production design. This concept, which Arbib named the

Pan American, so impressed Feldmann that he ordered a car to be built at a reported cost of some $10,000.

It was basically a detrimmed Series 250 convertible with a rakishly sectioned body accentuated by a jaunty "continental kit," modest chrome fins

above special round taillamps, a wide hood scoop, and an extended rear deck (Arbib had removed the back seat, deeming it unsuitable for a sports car).

Headlamp bezels and the inner grille section were predictively color-matched to the body's striking gold-green paint-work. Chrome wire wheels provided an appropriate finishing touch. The interior was basically stock except for different upholstery and a repositioned steering column.

As an obvious promotional tool for both Henney and Packard, the Pan American was booked for the March 1952 International Motor Sports Show in New York, for which Arbib moonlighted as art director. The hasty scheduling left no time to fit the planned hideaway cloth top, but nobody noticed. In fact, public reaction was so positive that Packard briefly hinted at a limited run for retail sale, only to demur after ordering just five copies, which Henney supplied with tops included.

The Pan American featured here is the show car, meaning it is first of the six cars built—and the only one without its intended folding top.

1952 Pontiac Chieftain Station Wagon

The 1952 Pontiacs sported the third in a series of styling updates to the basic circa-1949 design. A new grille, fresh trim, and redesigned wheel covers were the major appearance changes.

The slow-selling Streamliner fastbacks were discontinued, as were the price-leader business coupes. All models were now marketed as Chieftains and, depending on body style, standard, DeLuxe, and Super DeLuxe trim levels were available.

Station wagons continued to use the all-steel body that replaced the traditional "woody" during 1949. The steel body stampings were embossed and decorated to resemble the birch and mahogany wood work that had been used previously.

Chieftain wagons came in standard trim with three-row seating for eight passengers or as a DeLuxe model that had room for six on two rows of seats. Second- and third-row seats could be removed to allow for greater cargo-hauling flexibility.

The most important change for the 1952 Pontiacs may have been in the optional automatic transmission. Dubbed Dual-Range Hydra-Matic, the improved gearbox offered two drive positions and came paired with a new "economy" rear axle that used a 3.08:1 ratio.

The gear selector's left "DR" position

used four gears for reduced engine revolutions that helped increase fuel economy, provide quieter operation, and promote longer engine life. This range was best suited to highway or light-traffic use.

The right "DR" setting used only the first three gears to provide better acceleration and flexibility in heavy traffic. This position also increased engine braking when descending long hills or mountain roads. Selecting "Lo" allowed the car to start in second gear, a great advantage on icy roads.

The new Hydra-Matic was only available with new high-compression (7.7:1) versions of Pontiac's six- and eight-cylinder L-head engines. The high-compression head raised the six's output to 102 bhp from 100 and the eight to 122 bhp from 118. Cars equipped with the standard three-speed manual transmission came with the base engines.

Road tests of Pontiac Eights with the Dual-Range Hydra-Matic appeared in the April 1952 issues of *Motor Trend* and *Science and Mechanics*. Both spoke highly of the new transmission, with *MT* declaring it "undoubtedly the best compromise between the stick shift and the fluid coupling; it has the 'shifting ability' of one, combined with the ease in shifting of the other."

By far, Pontiac buyers preferred the eight-cylinder engine and the Dual-Range Hydra-Matic transmission. More than 90 percent of buyers chose the eight, and more than eight in 10 bought the automatic.

Readers may notice that the featured car wears a sunshade, fender skirts, lighted hood ornament, and extra brightwork including headlight rings and gravel shields that were not included in the Chieftain Eight wagon's $2689 base price.

1952 Siata 208S Spyder

In 1952, Fiat stepped out of its usual mass-market track to offer the 8V, a swoopy sports coupe with a 2.0-liter V-8 engine. Very soon, the engine began appearing in cars from a much smaller Italian automaker: Siata.

This sharing was no random act; it had a long history. Siata—the acronym for a company established to sell performance parts and tune cars—was founded in 1926 by an amateur racing driver named Giorgio Ambrosini. Perhaps because they both called Turin

home, Fiats drew most of Siata's attention, which fostered mutual ties.

Siata began making cars under its own name in the late Forties, many of them equipped with Fiat engines modified for additional performance. Out of this process came the 208S, powered by the 8V's ohv V-8, which, by some accounts, Siata helped to design.

The oversquare 8V engine featured an aluminum block and heads with wedge-shaped combustion chambers and inserted cylinder liners. Induction was through a pair of two-barrel Weber carburetors. With its high-revving short-stroke design and 7.5:1 compression ratio, the engine made 110 bhp in base form and 30-50 bhp more with Siata-designed

camshafts and better-breathing heads. This power was channeled through a five-speed manual gearbox.

The 106-inch-wheelbase 208S featured a box-section frame and four-wheel independent suspension made up of Fiat-derived components. Hydraulic drum brakes were used at all four corners, and 6.50×15 tires were

standard. The aluminum-body Spyder roadster had a top speed of around 110 mph. (A Vignale-bodied 208S America fastback coupe with hidden headlights and a tube frame was faster still with a reported top speed around 120 mph.) Spyders came with a top and side curtains for protection against the elements.

At approximately 2500 pounds and $5500 in the USA, the V-8 Siata was lighter and less expensive than contemporary 2.0-liter sports cars from Ferrari and Maserati. Perhaps predictably, the 208S attracted the attention of a number of sports car racers. Jack McAfee, the West Coast importer of Siatas, even prepared one for the 1953 Carrera

Panamericana, resleeving the cylinders to reduce displacement to 1.6 liters in order to enter a different class. Unfortunately, he crashed the car during the famed road race through Mexico.

The 208S was available until 1955. Siata moved on to other projects—among them the Mitzi two-cylinder mini-car before closing its doors in 1970.

1953 Cadillac Eldorado Convertible

The first Cadillac Eldorado cost almost double the price of a Series 62 convertible in 1953, yet Cadillac probably lost money on every one it sold because of the extensive special tooling required for a limited-production car. The Eldorado was based on a show car displayed in 1952 to commemorate Cadillac's 50th anniversary. The name Eldorado, from the Spanish el dorado, meaning "the gilded one," tied in with the marque's golden anniversary.

Because of the Korean War, there was no General Motors Motorama to show off that first Eldo in '52, but there was a Motorama tour in 1953 at which

to exhibit the production Eldorado, the Buick Skylark, and the Oldsmobile Fiesta—a trio of glamorous convertibles built to raise the image of their respective marques. Eldorado's reputation got a special boost when Dwight D. Eisenhower rode in one during his presidential inauguration parade on January 20, 1953. Most presidents-elect arrived at their inaugurations in dignified limousines or phaetons. Ike, with his unassuming and sunny persona, looked natural standing up in the back of an Eldorado.

Cadillac's image was already riding high. The Sixteen helped solidify Cadillac's reputation in the Thirties. Then, starting in 1949, a powerful ohv V-8 helped establish the brand as the top American luxury car for years to come. For '53, the 331-cid V-8 was rated at 210 bhp. That was probably understated because

Cadillac

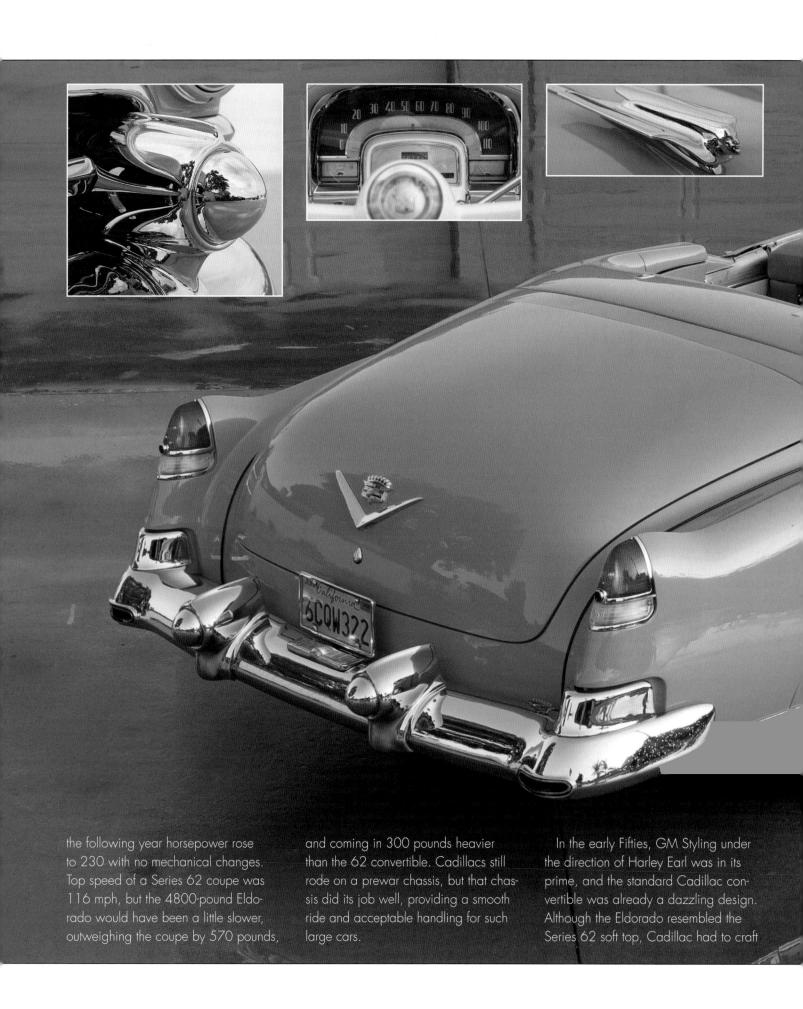

the following year horsepower rose to 230 with no mechanical changes. Top speed of a Series 62 coupe was 116 mph, but the 4800-pound Eldorado would have been a little slower, outweighing the coupe by 570 pounds,

and coming in 300 pounds heavier than the 62 convertible. Cadillacs still rode on a prewar chassis, but that chassis did its job well, providing a smooth ride and acceptable handling for such large cars.

In the early Fifties, GM Styling under the direction of Harley Earl was in its prime, and the standard Cadillac convertible was already a dazzling design. Although the Eldorado resembled the Series 62 soft top, Cadillac had to craft

a special hood, cowl, doors, and body shell for the Eldorado. Cadillac lowered the chassis an inch, and overall height was three inches lower. Mounted upon the lowered cowl was a panoramic windshield—a touch that spread to other Cadillac models in 1954. The doors had a sporting dip, and, when the top was folded, a metal cover neatly concealed it.

Chrome wire wheels were standard. Also standard were a four-speed Hydra-Matic transmission, power steering, whitewall tires, fog lights, power seat, signal-seeking radio, power windows, and windshield washers. A special leather-upholstered interior included a padded dash. The price for all this luxury was $7750, which 532 buyers considered acceptable. The Eldorado came back for 1954 but with specific bright trim applied to a body shell shared with the Series 62 convertible. While the '54 Eldorado wasn't as distinctive as the original, its price was slashed to $5738, which spurred sufficient sales to assure its survival.

1953 Chrysler Town & Country Station Wagon

Chrysler had a somewhat odd relationship with the station wagon. The brand didn't carry a factory sanctioned wagon until 1941, later than practically every other wagon producer, and when it did, it was a vehicle that was a curious cross between a sedan and wagon with a wood body, sloping steel roof, and dutch-door tailgate.

This mixed-style hauler was named Town & Country and it continued in this form as a 1942 model, but didn't return to the lineup after World War II. The Town & Country monicker stuck around, but it was applied to high-style "woody" sedans and convertibles.

It wasn't until 1949 that Chrysler returned to the station wagon fold, this time with a conventionally constructed wood-slathered T&C in the low-line

Royal series. A scant 850 of the nine-passenger vehicles were built, but that didn't deter the division. For 1950, it offered two kinds of Royal Town & Countrys—a wood-trimmed version and a cheaper all-steel variant. Respective sales were just 599 and 100 units, but they did include one significant advance in wagon design—a rear window that retracted into the tailgate instead of having to be propped up as a separate assembly.

As modest as sales were for T&Cs, Chrysler was in the station wagon business to stay. In fact, with the Royal gone, 1951 would see wagon offerings expand into the Windsor, Saratoga, and upscale New Yorker lines—all without a hint of wood.

By 1953, the year of our featured car, Chrysler was ready for fresh styling that featured more drawn-down hoods and wide, curved, undivided windshields that imparted a lighter, more airy

look. However, while sedan fenders looked more of a piece with the rear quarters, wagons still had obviously separate bolt-on fenders.

Town & Countrys were offered two ways: as a six-cylinder Windsor or as a V-8 New Yorker. In either case, they rode a 125.5-inch wheelbase and seated six—though a removable seat for children (the sales catalog showed it placed all the way at the back of the cargo compartment) was available at extra cost. With the split-folding second-row seats folded down, there was a cargo floor 75 inches long and 47 inches wide, and dropping the external-

ly hinged tailgate extended floor length to a maximum 116 inches.

The $3259 Windsor T&C accounted for 1242 sales, but 1399 customers laid out an additional $639 to step up to the New Yorker wagon. Why not, considering that the extra money bought the sensational 331-cid hemispherical-head "FirePower" V-8 that made 180 bhp and 312 pound-feet of torque.

1953 Dannenhauer
and Stauss Cabriolet

The automotive world would be a somewhat drearier place if not for the efforts of small "boutique" manufacturers. These tuners and coachbuilders take the familiar and make it special. They may start with somebody else's car, but where they end up is often fascinating.

That point is made here by Dannenhauer and Stauss, a coachbuilder in Stuttgart, Germany, that put dramatic new bodies with a distinct Porsche flavor on a Volkswagen platform. A veritable handful were built between 1951 and 1957—estimates range from 80 to 135—and there are few known

survivors. Today they excite a body of in-the-know VW enthusiasts.

Dannenhauer and Stauss was established in Stuttgart soon after World War II. (The firm still exists but is no longer involved in the automotive field.) Prior to the war, Gottfried Dannenhauer had worked for Reutter, which built bodies for the prototypes of what would become the Volkswagen Type 1.

Dannenhauer and son Kurt Stauss were anxious to build a distinctive sports car from VW mechanicals, but for its styling they turned to two outside designers with experience in aerodynamics. The manufacturing process was somewhat less technological. The majority of each body was pounded out by hand over wooden forms—just the doors, engine cover, and front cargo lid were industrial pressings.

Early cars had a divided windshield, but during '53 that was changed to single-pane glass. The car was lengthened at both ends and got a Porsche-type grille over the rear engine cover and a Porsche license-plate lamp that also housed the brakelight.

The body was lower than a VW Beetle's, so the seats were specially

made. Leather upholstery, like that found in our feature car, was an option. Interior components were borrowed liberally from the Volkswagen parts book, which naturally spawned updates. For instance, the '53s adopted the driver-centered speedometer, central chrome radio grille, and covered glove box.

Dannenhauer and Stauss cars weren't necessarily cheap. By one account, the body alone cost about as much as a complete Beetle sedan. Most were convertibles with a well-insulated top, but

perhaps fewer than five hardtop coupes were also built.

Some say VW's own sporty-looking Karmann-Ghia squelched demand for D&S cars. Today, 18 are known to exist, 13 of which (including a hardtop) are in drivable condition.

The owner of the Fjord Green 1953 Dannenhauer and Stauss cabriolet featured here replaced the original Volkswagen Beetle "eggbeater" with a 1.5-liter Porsche Super 1500 mill when the car was restored.

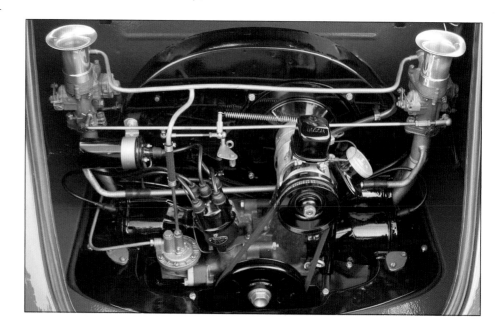

1953 Henry J Corsair Two-Door Sedan

Henry J. Kaiser revolutionized ship-building during World War II with his mass-produced Liberty ships. While Kaiser was building ships faster than anyone had ever imagined, he was already planning to shock the auto industry with a postwar "people's car." As early as 1942, Kaiser was concocting a front-wheel-drive, fiberglass-bodied car to sell for as little as $400. However, when the 1947 Kaiser took its bow, it was a conventional, medium-price sedan.

The realities of getting a car into production forced Kaiser to abandon his unorthodox ideas, but he never gave up on the idea of creating a people's car.

When a radical design for a tubular-framed economy car was presented to Kaiser, he jumped at it even though his chief engineer said it was impossible. The engineer was right and production cars were more conventional with a tra-ditional ladder frame. Willys provided engines, a 68-bhp, 134-cid four and an 80-bhp, 161-cid six; both flatheads. The four was Willys's "Go-Devil" engine that also powered Jeeps. Helped by a curb weight of only 2293 pounds, the Henry J delivered fuel economy in the mid to high twenties.

Kaiser stylists and consulting designer Howard "Dutch" Darrin didn't like the fastback body and offered other proposals. Those proposals were rejected, but

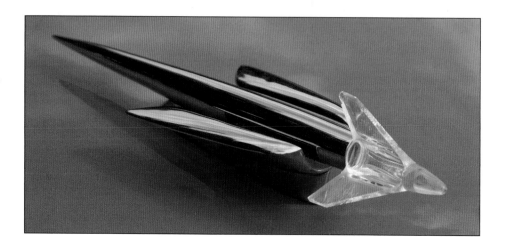

Darrin was asked to assist the in-house styling team in refining the selected design.

Kaiser-Frazer Corporation ran a name-the-car contest, but that was a PR stunt since the company knew from the beginning the car would be named in honor of the boss. The new compact made its debut in 1951 as the Henry J. Although a separate make, the letter "K" appeared in several places on the car as a reminder that the Henry J was a Kaiser product. Prices started at a reasonable $1219 for the four and $1343 for the six.

Road testers of the time thought the car was lively with good handling. Tom McCahill, driving a six, did 0-60 mph in 14.8 seconds and reported a top speed of 84 mph. For comparison, in *Motor Trend* tests, a '51 Ford V-8 automatic went from zero to 60 in 17.82

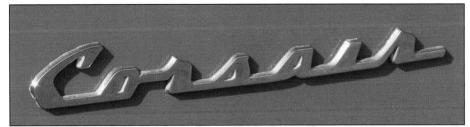

seconds and topped out at 87.25. Henry J performance was quite good for an economy car; however, one complaint was that it was too spartan, lacking a glove box, dome light, and opening trunklid. At first, a folding rear seat was the only access to the trunk. Initial acceptance was good, with nearly 82,000 sold for the 1951 model year, but then declined rapidly. Nineteen fifty-four would be the last year for Henry J.

Our featured car is a four-cylinder 1953 Henry J Corsair that cost $1399 new. By '53, a glove box and dome light were standard. Henry Js also gained an opening trunklid, but the folding rear seat became optional. This car is equipped with the optional "Dinosaur Vinyl" upholstery. Kaiser's head of color and trim, Carleton Spencer, created this alligator-grain vinyl that proved extremely tough and long wearing.

1953 Mercury Monterey Convertible Coupe

Nineteen fifty-three proved to be a big year for Mercury for a number of reasons. It would be difficult to find a better souvenir of that successful season than the Monterey convertible seen here.

Though 1953 Mercs wore facelifted styling on the slab-sided bodies that had been brand new the year before, model-year production shot up. The end of government-imposed strategic-materials restrictions for the Korean War allowed automakers to resume full operation, and Mercury turned out 305,863 cars for the second-best model year in the

marque's 14-year history. Finally, a Monterey convertible produced that September was celebrated as the 40-millionth U.S.-built Ford Motor Company vehicle.

Mercury bowed its first formal two-series line for 1953: the Custom series offered a two-door hardtop and two- and four-door sedans, while the top-line Monterey line listed a convertible,

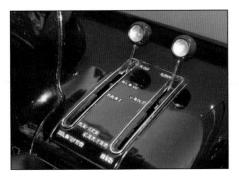

hardtop, wagon, and four-door sedan. Exterior appearance was touched up with the addition of a full-length body-side spear that helped give the cars a longer, more integrated look. Retained from 1952 was a trendy dashboard with big aircraft-type levers flanking a large half-moon gauge cluster.

Mercury models rode a 118-inch wheelbase, and were powered by a 255.4-cid "flathead" V-8 engine that was good for 125 horsepower and could be paired with an optional three-speed Merc-O-Matic automatic transmission. A modern overhead-valve V-8 engine would replace the aging flathead in the 1954 models.

This Monterey droptop wears Siren Red paint, which was one of three new colors available only on station wagons and convertibles. Siren Red was also the color used on the Monterey convertible

selected for the 40-millionth domestic FoMoCo commemorative car.

All of the 8463 Monterey convertibles built for 1953 benefited from a new roof mechanism that allowed for faster raising and lowering the of the folding top. The featured ragtop is equipped with the power steering, power brakes, and power seat that became optionally available late in the run. These extras would have boosted the car's $2390 starting price. Other extra-cost items on this car include Merc-O-Matic, power windows, a radio, and the road lamps beneath the front bumper guards.

1954 Ford Customline Two-Door Sedan

The 1954 Ford was a pivot point for its manufacturer. On one hand, it carried over the styling—albeit facelifted—the body styles, and the series names in place since 1952. On the other hand, the '54 ushered in certain engineering and detail changes that would live on in it successors.

Foremost among the changes was the switch from Ford's long-serving "flathead" V-8 to a completely modern short-stroke overhead-valve mill. Dubbed the "Y-block" because of its deep crankcase, it displaced the same 239.4 cubic inches as the engine it replaced, but generated 130 horsepower, 20 more than its forebearer. This was easily the hottest engine in the low-price field, but it would grow larger and more powerful over the next few years. The new V-8 was standard in the Sunliner convertible and optional in all other models for about $80.

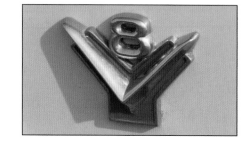

This was also the year that a ball-joint front suspension, already proven in Lincolns, was adopted to improve ride and handling. It was accompanied by a half-inch wheelbase extension. The resulting 115.5-inch span served Fords through 1956.

Then, too, 1954 was the year of the "Astra-Dial" speedometer, which admitted natural light through the rear of the speedometer housing to illuminate the dial. The feature continued into 1955.

Another of the year's highlights was the first Skyliner, a Victoria two-door hardtop with a Plexiglass roof insert. This feature was available through 1956. Other new models for 1954 included a two-door Ranch Wagon in the midrange Customline series and a four-door sedan in the top-of-the-line Crestline series.

The Customline two-door sedan was the best selling 1954 Ford with 293,375 built. The base price of the V-8-powered Customline two-door sedan was $1820, but that didn't cover options like the $41 power brakes that are on the Seamist Green car featured here.

It's worth noting that Chevrolet and Plymouth trailed Ford by a full year in offering a powerful, lightweight V-8 engine. And as styling and engineering were essentially carryover for all the low-price three in 1954, the new engine was undoubtedly the single most important factor in putting Ford on top in the industry production totals with a tally of 1,165,942 cars. The margin over Chevy was slim to be sure—less than 23,000 units for the model year—but it was an important moral victory and an indication of just how far Ford Motor Company had come in a very short period of time.

In fact, Dearborn was now solidly entrenched as the world's second largest automaker, having passed Chrysler Corporation in 1951—and this despite only having three makes on the market to GM and Chrysler's five. Much of this success was directly attributable to the Ford line.

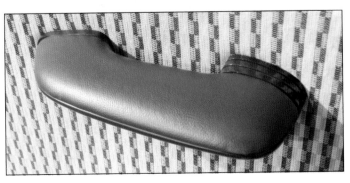

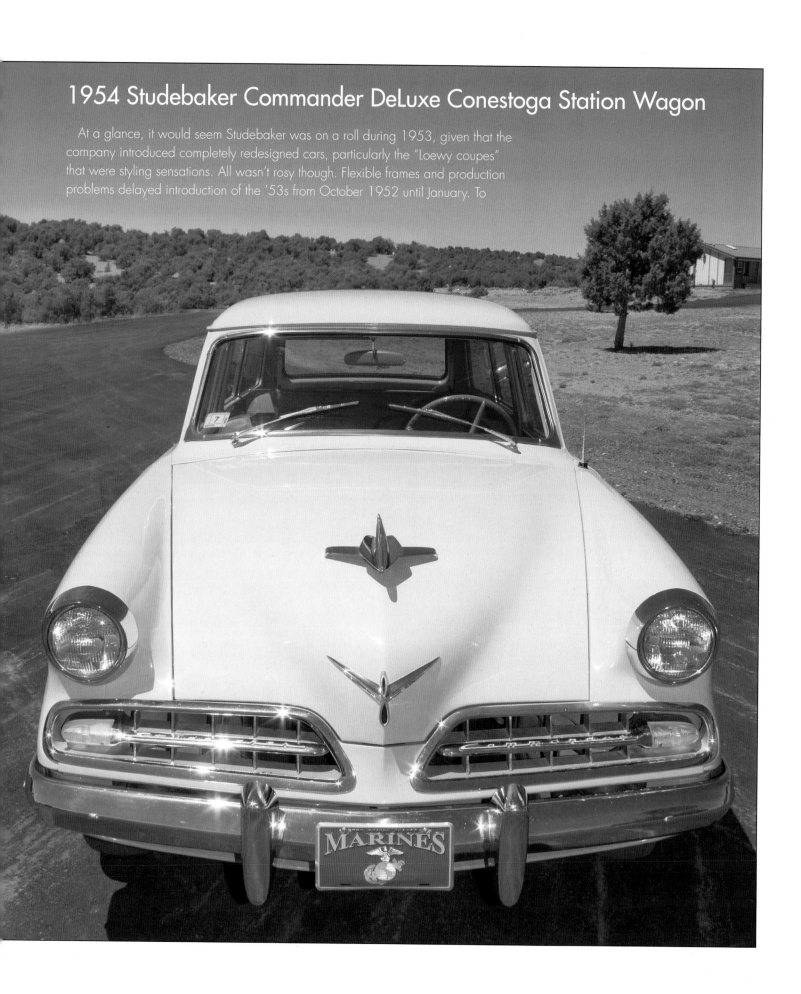

1954 Studebaker Commander DeLuxe Conestoga Station Wagon

At a glance, it would seem Studebaker was on a roll during 1953, given that the company introduced completely redesigned cars, particularly the "Loewy coupes" that were styling sensations. All wasn't rosy though. Flexible frames and production problems delayed introduction of the '53s from October 1952 until January. To compound the difficulties, the company couldn't meet better-than-expected coupe demand while the not-as-stylish sedans weren't as popular as the company projected. In the end, production for the model year came to 169,899, less than half the peak total of 343,164 just three years before.

The big news for 1954 was the addition of a station wagon to the line, a steel-bodied two-door called Conestoga. The name paid tribute to Studebaker's

original horse-drawn Conestoga wagons of late 1800s, the "prairie schooners" that helped settle the American West. These new wagons were best suited to shuttling families around fast-developing suburbia.

Like Studebaker's sedans—save the long-wheelbase Commander Land Cruiser—the station wagons rode a 116.5-inch span. Conestogas were offered in both the Champion and Commander series, with each available in DeLuxe and tonier Regal trim.

While Champions came with the old 170-cid L-head inline six rated at 85 bhp, Commanders used Studebaker's

modern ohv V-8. The 232.6-cube engine was good for 127 horsepower, seven more than it had in 1953. Either engine could be mated to a three-speed manual gearbox—with or without overdrive—or a Borg-Warner-built automatic transmission.

Inside, Conestogas had two rows of seats and could carry up to six passengers. The rear seat could be folded flat to increase cargo space. Out back, a two-piece tailgate included a flip-up rear window.

The 1954 Conestoga featured here is a Commander DeLuxe, Studebaker's least-expensive V-8 wagon, with a base

price of $2448. When photographed, the odometer on this original-condition example read 13,303.3 miles.

Despite better assembly quality and the addition of the wagon body style, Studebaker deliveries for 1954 fell by more than half to 81,930.

On October 1, 1954, Packard purchased Studebaker. Studebaker sales improved in '55, but both companies lost their independence. Packard disappeared after 1958. Studebaker's South Bend, Indiana, plant was shuttered just before Christmas 1963. The final Studebakers were built in early 1966 at the firm's small Canadian factory.

1955 Chrysler New Yorker Deluxe Town & Country Station Wagon

In the early Fifties, Chrysler cars had the engineering, size, and assembly quality to compete with Lincolns, Buicks, and Cadillacs. However, in the styling department, they were decidedly dowdy. Chrysler Chairman K. T. Keller had dictated the conservative appearance, but after suffering through the rough sales environment of 1953 and 1954, he finally admitted to the *Detroit Free Press*, "I have seen the error of my ways."

Designer Virgil Exner was given the task of styling all of the corporation's 1955 offerings. When the new models were introduced in fall 1954, they were dramatic departures from the ho-hum cars they replaced. Chrysler admen said Exner's fleet of beauties displayed "The Forward Look," and the copy of one

brochure described the new look as a "fresh, new, and contemporary approach to car design."

The new Chryslers evolved from Exner creations that first appeared in 1952: the Ghia-built Chrysler K-310 show car and the special dual-cowl Imperial parade phaetons built for Detroit, Los Angeles, and New York. Lower and sleeker than the cars they replaced, the line was touted as the "100-Million-Dollar Look." Some said this claim was a reference to the approximate amount Chrysler spent transforming its entire 1955 lineup.

Shoppers drawn to Chrysler showrooms by the attractive styling found a simplified lineup. At introduction, only Windsor Deluxe and New Yorker Deluxe models were available in two-door hardtop, convertible, four-door sedan,

and station-wagon body styles. The slow-selling club coupes and long-wheelbase eight-passenger sedan were nowhere to be found. Then, during the year, the high-performance—and soon-to-be-legendary—C-300 hardtop joined the roster.

While all rode a 126-inch wheelbase, engine offerings varied by the series. Windsors used a new 300.5-cid "Spitfire" V-8. It had polyspherically shaped combustion chambers and was rated at 188 bhp. New Yorkers had a 331.1-cid "Firepower" mill with hemispherical combustion chambers that was good for 250 ponies. The C-300 had a unique version of the "hemi" tuned for 300 horses.

Wagons continued to bear the Town & Country name. They came two ways: The Windsor started at $3332 and the New Yorker listed for a princely $4209. (For the sake of reference, Buick's most

expensive '55 wagon, the Century Estate, began at $3175.)

The year was a record one for the industry, but the public still must have appreciated the new Chrysler styling. Production of 152,777 units was an increase of more than 45 percent over the previous season's dismal tally. With the 1955s, Chrysler Corporation began to assert itself as one of the industry's styling leaders.

The 1955 New Yorker Deluxe Town & Country featured here is one of the 1036 built. Options on the Canyon Tan and Desert Sand wagon include power steering, a four-way power seat, and heater. The chrome wire wheels are a period factory extra added to the car, and there is also a mysterious holster that a previous owner added underneath the driver's seat.

1955 Hudson Hornet Hollywood Hardtop Coupe

Loyalists who stuck with Hudson after its 1954 merger with Nash had to get used to some changes in their marque of choice. Consolidation of assembly in Nash plants spelled the end of Hudson's signature "Step-down" bodies. For 1955, they were replaced by modified Nash unitized bodies, available only in two-door hardtop and four-door sedan styles. Hudson also shared Nash's shorter 114.25- and 121.25-inch wheelbases, switched to rear coil springs, and adopted some different powertrain features. Hudson owners were introduced to Nash features like "Twin Travel Bed" seats and air conditioning with the works confined to under the hood.

However, Hudson partisans could still find familiar touchstones in these new cars, particularly in '55. Six-cylinder models continued to sport L-head Hudson-designed engines, including the 308-cid Hornet mill that made 170 bhp when equipped with the Twin H-Power dual-carburetor manifold. The "Triple Safe" brake system, a Hudson feature since 1936, was continued,

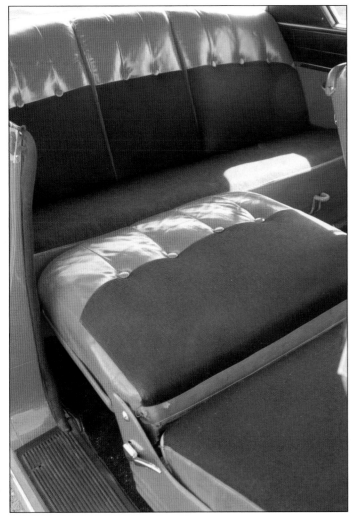

too. While Nash doors opened with a squeeze of their flat handles, entry to Hudsons still required gripping a loop-style handle and depressing a thumb button. The thick grille frame incorporated parking/turn-signal lamps at its lower ends as in previous years; the grille's eggcrate surface was picked up from a '55 Step-down facelift Hudson had in the works before the merger. Series-identification badges and the trunk ornament were carried over from '54. So were the instrument cluster and steering wheel.

What was new to both American Motors brands in 1955 was V-8 power, in this case a Packard-built 320-cid ohv engine with two-barrel carburetion rated at 208 bhp. Cars with this engine were hooked to Packard's Twin Ultramatic automatic transmission. The V-8 power-team in a 121.25-inch-wheelbase Hudson Hornet added $255–$265 to the cost of a six-cylinder job with the standard three-speed manual transmission and, as *Motor Trend* discovered, delivered 0-60-mph acceleration in 12.1 seconds and a top speed of around 105 mph.

Thanks in part to an introduction that was delayed until February 1955, production of full-sized Hudsons tumbled by 44 percent from '54. Thus, factory output of some models was particularly low. For instance, just 1770 Hornet Custom Hollywood V-8 hardtops were built. Driving comfort of our featured example is enhanced by the optional air conditioner, power windows, and power steering—the last a feature *Motor Trend* heartily endorsed after testing a '55 Hudson without it.

The distinctly Hudson elements of these hybrid "Hashes"—grille design, six-cylinder engines, etc.—started slipping away in 1956. Indeed, Hudson itself was rapidly fading, its name destined to be stricken from the roster of American automakers just a year later.

1956 DeSoto Firedome Seville Hardtop Sedan

Chrysler products of the early Fifties were finely engineered, but unfortunately the cars looked like they had been styled by engineers, too. The visual part of the equation—likely the most important piece on the showroom floor—was addressed for 1955. The corporation's cars evolved from frumpy to Fifties fabulous thanks to Director of Styling Virgil Exner's "Forward Look."

DeSoto benefited as much as any of the five brands from this process.

Push Button Driving...

It's simple, easy, effortless. Here's all you do:

1. Push the "N" button all the way.
2. Start the engine.

Select the driving range you want by simply pushing the appropriate button.

ALWAYS BE SURE YOU PUSH THE BUTTON ALL THE WAY SO THAT IT STAYS IN.

Buttons are illuminated for night driving. With new push button control, you touch and GO!

Happy Driving!

Though its overall size hadn't changed much from 1954, appearance was dramatically different and the cars looked longer, lower, and wider. The design extended to careful selection of interior and exterior colors as well.

This was the era of the expected annual styling change, and for '56, DeSoto didn't disappoint. Up front, the marque's traditional toothy grille was replaced with a mesh unit suspended from vertical towers that looked much like bumper guards but actually housed the turn signals.

The big news was out back. As he did to all of Chrysler's 1956 offerings,

Exner added tailfins. The fins began near the rear window and gracefully rose in a straight line as they extended to the end of the fender. Viewed from the rear, the peaked fin formed the top of a forward-leaning bright-metal panel that housed three vertically stacked circular taillamp lenses. DeSoto marketers called this arrangement the "Control Tower." Meanwhile, a new rear bumper blended smoothly with the reworked fenders.

The fins transformed the DeSoto's rear end, adding a sense of drama where the original rear fender and taillamp treatment had been somewhat generic in comparison. The color-sweep areas on the bodysides were revised at the rear as well, with the upper molding helping to define the lower edge of the fin.

Other talking points were minor. They included a 12-volt electrical system, improved brakes, gas-fired heater, and an optional Highway Hi-Fi record player.

The DeSoto lineup expanded for '56 thanks to the addition of a four-door hardtop body style that was available in both DeSoto series. There were two Firedome four-door hardtops—the $2833 Seville and a better-trimmed Sportsman that listed for $120 more. Each came standard with a 230-bhp version of DeSoto's 330-cid "hemi-head" V-8. In the top-of-the-line Fireflite series, the new four-door hardtop was only sold as a Sportsman. It priced from $3431. Its version of the 330 V-8 had a four-barrel carburetor and made 255 horsepower.

Of the three new four-door hardtops, the lowest-priced Firedome Seville proved most popular, with deliveries totaling 4030. The Fireflite Sportsman rang up 3350 sales, and the Firedome Sportsman another 1645.

Our featured car is a 1956 Firedome Seville four-door hardtop that except for an exterior repaint largely remains in original condition.

1956 Ford
Fairlane Victoria
Hardtop Coupe

For 1956, Ford tried to sell safety. In hindsight that's surprising given the public's mid-Fifties preoccupation with performance and styling. Luckily for Ford dealers, the company also delivered more horsepower and freshened looks.

Ford called its package of safety features "Lifeguard Design." The main goal of the campaign was to reduce or prevent injuries in the event of a collision, mostly through what we would now call passive safety.

Ford engineers along with university and U.S. Air Force researchers concentrated their efforts in the passenger compartment. Dash knobs were redesigned so they protruded less than they had in '55, and a deep-dish steering wheel was added. Both changes were aimed at reducing the chance of impalement.

Other tweaks included a front-seat locking mechanism meant to keep the seat from sliding forward in a quick stop. Stronger door latches were intended to keep the doors closed and passengers inside the car during a crash. Additional Lifeguard features

were available at extra cost, including a padded dashboard and sunvisors, a shatter-resistant rearview mirror, and airplane-style lap belts.

The public didn't wildly embrace Lifeguard Design, but even so Ford's seatbelt supplier couldn't keep up with demand. In the end, only about one in five '56 Fords had seatbelts. Further-

more, Ford research indicated less than 20 percent of the people who bought the belts used them; the bottom line was something like four percent of '56 Ford drivers buckled up.

On the styling front, Ford worked up a tasteful update of the 1955 model, itself a clever redo of the circa-1952 body. Changes for '56 included a new grille,

elliptical parking lamps in large housings, more prominent headlamp bezels and side trim, and enlarged taillamps.

Most closed cars received lowered roof stampings, but the Victoria hardtop benefited from a more dramatic change. When Ford introduced the flashy Fairlane Crown Victoria in 1955, it featured a lower, longer roof panel and a completely different rear window than the regular 1955 Victoria hardtop. The unique roofline helped the Crown Vic's otherwise-unchanged body look longer and lower, both very desirable selling points at the time. For 1956, Ford expanded the use of the Crown Victoria's sleeker roofline to Victoria hardtops in both the Customline and Fairlane series.

A six was still standard in '56 Fords, but V-8s were available in three sizes: 272, 292, and 312 cid. Horsepower ranged from 173 for a two-barrel 272 up to 225 for a hot "Thunderbird Special" 312. Our featured Fairlane Victoria packs a 215-horse 312 V-8 backed by a three-speed manual transmission with optional overdrive.

1956 Maserati A6G 2000GT Coupe

While the Maserati nameplate has been part of the automotive world since the Twenties, the five car-building Maserati brothers initially busied themselves solely with competition machines. It wasn't until after World War II that the marque's trident logo appeared on roadgoing grand tourers.

By the mid Fifties, Maserati was starting to hit its stride, as evidenced by the A6G 2000GT coupe that is seen here. The 2000 was the beneficiary of a double-overhead-camshaft six-cylinder engine that greatly enhanced performance. Meanwhile, a number of Italy's leading coachbuilders contributed lovely body designs. Among them was the shop of Allemano from Turin, which fashioned the body of the featured car.

The Maserati on these pages wasn't actually the handiwork of any of the Maserati brothers. In 1938, they sold out to industrialist Adolfo Orsi, who moved the operation from the Maseratis' native Bologna to Modena. When their service contract with Orsi expired at the end of 1947, the three surviving brothers moved on to form OSCA—the Maserati name remained the property of their former employer.

Shortly before their departure, though, Ernesto Maserati had worked up a roadable 1.5-liter ohc six-cylinder sports car, the A6. The Orsi-controlled Maserati works put 65-bhp two-seat A6 coupes

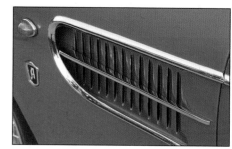

and convertibles on sale in 1948. Three years later, a 2.0-liter ohc six was fitted into a second-generation car known as the A6G. It made 100 horsepower. Produced by the handful into 1954, the A6G enjoyed the attentions of coach-builders Frua, Farina, Vignale, Ghia, and Bertone.

It was at the 1954 Paris Salon that Maserati first showed the next evolution of the A6, the A6G 2000. Its distinguishing technical feature was an engine that, while still a 2.0-liter and fed by triple Weber carburetors, was completely different from its predecessor. For starters, it was a dohc design. Where the prior model's cylinder dimensions were undersquare, the 2000's were oversquare (and displacement was 31cc greater). With 150 bhp at 6000 rpm, it moved this latest A6G to 60 mph in 10 seconds; top speed was said to be about 130 mph.

Like earlier A6s, the 2000 utilized a four-speed transmission, recirculating-ball steering, and hydraulic drum brakes all around. Independent coil-spring suspension in front and a solid rear axle with leaf springs were continued, as was the 100.4-inch wheelbase, but wider 6.00×16 tires now wrapped around the Borrani wire wheels. Body-on-tubular-frame construction was another carry-over feature.

Regardless of which carrozzeria handled the styling, the 2000 had a lower, wider interpretation of the divided Maserati grille. Just 60 examples of the A6G 2000 were built through 1957. The featured car is one of the 21 Allemano-bodied coupes produced during that run.

1956 Oldsmobile Super 88 Holiday Hardtop Sedan

It's hard to believe that the car on these pages is original from the tires up. This 1956 Oldsmobile Super 88 Holiday four-door hardtop was purchased by an elderly lady in Kentucky and used by her housekeeper for shopping. A nephew inherited the car, but didn't drive it—although he did start the engine occasionally before selling it.

Low mileage is one of the secrets of the Olds's eternally young look: There are only 6700 miles on the car, which has required no mechanical or cosmetic work. Even the tires—again original—are in surprisingly good condition.

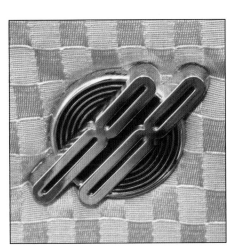

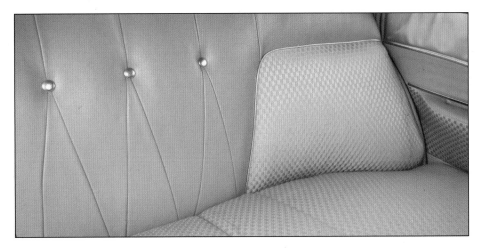

When new, there was no need to baby the Olds Super 88. *Science and Mechanics* magazine clocked 0-60 mph in 10.2 seconds and stated that the Olds "clobbers the 11.4+ seconds averaged by the seven 1956 test cars we have tested so far this year." In a Q & A format for its '56 buyer's guide, *Motor Trend* praised it this way: "Q. Does it [Oldsmobile] have good performance?

A. Almost a superfluous question—it's an Olds, and the already-hot Rocket engine has been boosted in horsepower. A real delight for the would-be dragster. . . ."

The boost in horsepower was the result of an increase in the compression ratio from 1955's 8.5:1 to 9.5:1 for '56. The horsepower rating of Oldsmobile's ohv Rocket V-8 engine used in the Super 88 jumped from 202 to 240.

Top speed was estimated to be 110 to 113 mph. The Rocket V-8 of our featured car is mated to a new-for-'56 Jetaway Hydra-Matic Drive automatic transmission. For $15 more than Olds's base Hydra-Matic, Jetaway added a second fluid coupling for smoother operation as well as a "Park" position in the quadrant that eliminated the need to apply the parking brake.

Just as Olds had massaged the powertrain for '56, it also revised styling with a new concave grille. The Holiday two-door hardtop had been joined by a four-door Holiday in '55. By '56, the hardtop sedan was the most popular body style in the Super 88 range with 61,192 sold at $2881 to start.

The Super 88 was in the middle of Oldsmobile's three-series lineup. The base 88 and Super 88 shared a 122-inch wheelbase. The Super boasted better trim and 10 more horsepower. The Ninety-Eight rode a 126-inch wheelbase and had standard power steering and Jetaway transmission. The Super 88 had the best power-to-weight ratio of the three, which would have allowed this car's first driver to make quick work of these shopping trips.

1956 Packard Clipper Custom Four-Door Sedan

Packard's hard-driving president, James Nance, was determined to reestablish Packard in the luxury field. To do that he planned a long-overdue separation of Packard's luxury and medium-priced lines. A new model name was needed for the lower-price line, and the Clipper name from the Forties was resurrected for the job.

While the company worked feverishly to challenge Cadillac, some might think that Clipper models were neglected. That wasn't the case because the engineering and styling revolutions of the senior Packards were shared by Clippers.

Packard's smooth, reliable, straight eights were the luxury-car standard in the Twenties and Thirties, but Cadillac's high-compression ohv V-8 set the pace in the postwar world. For '55, Packard brought out its own ohv V-8 and beat Cadillac in the horsepower race. Clippers used a smaller version of the V-8. Still, with 352 cid and 275 bhp, the '56 Clipper Custom had the biggest, most powerful engine in its price range.

Perhaps Packard's most successful engineering advance was the self-leveling Torsion-Level front and rear torsion-bar suspension. Packard not only had the best ride but was considered by many to be the best-handling American car of its time. To demonstrate the new suspension, a Lincoln, a Cadillac, and a new Packard were driven over a rough railroad crossing. The Lincoln was damaged, the Cadillac bounced, but the Packard took it in stride.

Styling was perked up with a wrap-around windshield, new grille, and—on '56 Clippers—a broad band for two-tone color running along the body sides and "boomerang" taillights that became a favorite with customizers.

Clipper was a separate make briefly in early '56, with Packard's trademark red hexagon in the center of the ship's-wheel badge the only visible clue to Clipper's parentage. Dealers objected, and Packard script reappeared on the decklid at midyear.

The 1955-56 Packards and Clippers were great cars that should have saved the company, but the new cars were built in a new factory. Both factory and cars had teething problems that lead to severe delivery shortages and quality problems among the 1955 models.

The 1956 models were a fine package, but sales were worse than ever, and quality-control problems continued. For 1957, once-proud Packard was reduced to being a retrimmed Studebaker President with '56 Clipper taillights. After 1958 Packard was gone.

1957 Buick Century Convertible Coupe

Twenty-one years after its introduction, the Buick Century was still playing its historic role as a "banker's hot rod." The Century series bowed in '36 when Buick dropped its biggest engine in a smaller chassis.

Thanks to the resulting power-to-weight ratio, the Century name was no idle boast: By its second season, the car could do 100 mph. The same formula still worked in 1957, when the Century shared its 122-inch wheelbase with the entry-level Special but had the more powerful engine of the larger Super and

over the Special. By comparison, the standard Cadillac engine of that year produced the same 300 bhp and was only one cubic inch bigger.

To make the most of that power, Buick had recently improved its smooth, but formerly sluggish, Dynaflow automatic transmission for faster acceleration. With this powerteam, *Motor Trend* timed the 0-60-mph sprint in a '57 Century at 10.1 seconds. Meanwhile, handling was better thanks to a lower ride height and Buick's first ball-joint front suspension—though "better" is a relative term as this was a Fifties Buick with a suspension tuned more for a soft boulevard ride than sports car handling.

Buick had new bodies for '57 that were longer and lower, yet carried over the styling themes of recent years to maintain continuity. Just in case the changes were so subtle that one didn't recognize a new Buick, the badge on the center of the grille proudly proclaimed "1957."

Making use of the General Motors B-body shell, the 4085 Century convertibles built for 1957 had a curb weight of 4234 pounds and priced from $3598 in standard trim.

Roadmaster series. *Motor Life* estimated a top speed well beyond the century mark at 125 mph.

All '57 Buicks had a 364-cid ohv V-8. The Century and bigger Buicks had a four-barrel carburetor and 10.0:1 compression ratio that produced 300 bhp—a 50-horsepower advantage

The Century convertible featured on these pages includes an optional Sonomatic radio that the driver was able to tune using a floor-mounted pedal to seek the next station. Other extras on this "banker's hot rod" include power assist for brakes, steering, front seat, windows, and radio antenna.

1957 Chevrolet Two-Ten Four-Door Sedan

When the 1957 Chevrolet Two-Ten four-door sedan seen here was photographed, it had never been titled more than 40 miles from where it was built. It came from Chevrolet's Janesville, Wisconsin, plant. On Christmas Eve 1956, a Jefferson, Wisconsin, dealer sold the car to a schoolteacher from nearby Helenville, Wisconsin (35 miles from Janesville). In 2003, a man from Rockford, Illinois (36 miles from Janesville), purchased the Chevy from the teacher's estate.

The first owner always garaged the car and it was probably not driven after 1986. When ownership transferred in 2003, the car was in excellent original condition with only 59,985 miles on the odometer. The interior and paint on the roof are original. The lower body has been repainted and the engine rebuilt. The hardest part of restoration was finding only unused vintage factory parts.

In '57 Chevrolet offered an enlarged version of its small-block V-8 with 283 cid. This car has the tried and true 265-cid V-8 that was only available with a manual transmission in '57. A rare option is this car's padded dashboard.

The Two-Ten sedan was Chevrolet's best selling model in 1957 with 260,401 built. Top-trim Bel Air hardtop coupes and convertibles may be the most commonly seen models today, but in '57 it was the midrange Two-Ten sedans that were in the most driveways.

In 1957 Chevrolet was in the third year with this body shell, while Ford and Plymouth were completely restyled. Chevrolet might have had the same bodies that came out in 1955, but a $50 million facelift made it seem fresh.

Chevy's '57 facelift was carefully detailed for a longer, lower look, which wasn't an illusion. Cowl height was reduced with a new ventilation system featuring fresh-air intakes in the headlamp eyebrows feeding long, concealed ducts to the interior, one of the car's more radical features. This led to a lower hood, with twin "lance-shaped" windsplits instead of a central ornament. The new bumper/grille was dominated by a thick horizontal bar with a large Chevy crest in the center and small round parking lamps at each end, set against a mesh background.

Elsewhere, the '57 not only looked different than the '56 but, to most eyes,

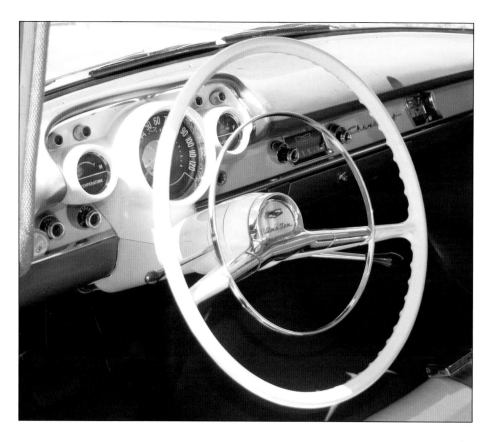

better. Two-Tens, like our featured car, wore bodyside trim made up of a full-length strip that split under the rear side window into a wedge, with the inner area painted to match roof color on two-tone cars. Out back were reshaped fenders that incorporated modest blade fins which helped keep up with the competition. Inside, there was a new asymmetrical "Command Post" dashboard and revised seat and door panel trim.

In spite of Chevrolet's best efforts, the restyled Ford was the best selling car in America for the '57 model year. (Chevrolet claimed to be the best seller for the calendar year, but that included early 1958 cars.) Posterity has been kinder to the '57 Chevy. Its combination of timeless styling and performance has made it a favorite with collectors for decades, and many consider the 1957 Chevy the definitive Fifties car.

1957 Ford Fairlane 500 Sunliner Convertible

Riding the competitive advantage of an all-new and attractive design, Ford was able to produce America's best-selling 1957 automobile. The push to deliver 1.67 million copies of its expanded lineup included significant contributions from two body styles that had historically been segment-leading sellers for Ford: station wagons and convertibles.

The five wagon offerings in the '57 Ford catalog tallied a brand-record 321,170 assemblies, or 19.4 percent of all that year's full-sized Fords. Convertibles, too, reached a new peak. The 77,726 traditional fabric-topped Fairlane 500 Sunliners added up to the clear favorite in the field. However, 1957 was the year that Ford added the Skyliner with a metal top that could be retracted under the car's uniquely shaped decklid. Another 20,766 Ford owners signed up for this mechanized marvel. With more than 98,000 droptops in circulation, Ford outsold the next three largest '57 convertible producers—Chevrolet, Oldsmobile, and Buick—combined!

Nineteen fifty-seven Fords came in two sizes, but even the "small" 116-inch-wheelbase sedans and wagons were longer and lower than their predecessors. Fairlanes and Fairlane 500s were on a 118-inch stretch, and featured more dramatic styling thanks to thin canted fins that flared out of the rear quarter panels. (Customs and Custom 500s had more subdued fins and a smaller rear bumper than the higher-series cars.)

Underneath everything was a redesigned frame that was about a foot wider midway down the frame rails. Underslung cross members earned the chassis the nickname "cowbelly" but they also allowed for floor pans to nestle between the frame rails. This permitted designers to lower the car while maintaining decent passenger room. Revised ball-joint front suspension, outboard mounted rear springs, and 14-inch-diameter wheels (which replaced 15-inchers) were new as well.

Reverse-canted A-pillars replaced the vertical windshield posts of 1955-56. A new instrument panel featured a fan-style speedometer. Closed-body Fairlane 500s featured nylon-and-vinyl upholstery and loop carpeting but the Sunliner had all-vinyl trim in a choice of four color combinations, and color-keyed vinyl-rubber floor covering.

When new, the Flame Red and Raven Black Sunliner featured here started at $2605, but it is packed with options that would have added about $600 to the delivered price. Most notable of the extra-cost items is the "Thunderbird Special" 312-cid V-8. (Fairlanes came with a choice of a 223-cid inline six or 292-cube V-8 as standard equipment.) With a four-barrel carb and dual exhausts, it makes 245 bhp. It is hooked to an optional Fordomatic three-speed automatic transmission. Appearance and protection extras include a continental kit and fender skirts.

1957 Mercedes-Benz 220S Convertible Coupe

This 1957 Mercedes-Benz 220S cabriolet looks much different from when it was discovered on an M-B dealer's lot in 1980 with a badly rusted trunk section, the wrong engine, and its suspension control arm embedded in the asphalt. Now it's an attractive, fun-to-drive parade car.

Like other automakers after World War II, Mercedes's first postwar car was a prewar model. It wasn't until 1951 that M-B brought out all-new cars. The 300 series was the prestige range with a flagship sedan and, later, the high-performance 300SL. The smaller, less expensive 220 was closely related to

the 300. Each was powered by an ohc six from a successful engine family that would be in production through 1972. The 220 used a smaller 2.2-liter version. It was mated to four-speed manual transmission with column shift. The chassis was advanced for the Fifties with full independent suspension; the rear suspension utilized swing axles. However, the 220 retained separate

196

The two-door models rode a 106.3-inch wheelbase that was 4.7 inches shorter than the sedan. For the 220S, the six gained dual carburetors and produced 112 bhp. Top speed was around 100 mph and 0-60 mph was achieved in 15-17 seconds.

Although not a hot rod, the 220S was one of the more elegant convertibles of the late Fifties. The interior was covered in leather and wood veneer, and this well-crafted luxury had a price. The 220S cabriolet cost $7138—about the same as a Cadillac Eldorado Biarritz convertible in '57.

In 1957, Mercedes hoped to expand its sales in the United States. To support this, parent company Daimler-Benz signed a distribution agreement with Studebaker-Packard Corporation. The current-day American branch, Mercedes-

body-on-frame construction until the envelope-body 220a sedan introduced in spring 1954 shifted to a unitized platform. Convertible bodies were still made the prewar way with steel panels over a wood frame.

During 1956 the 220 gave way to the more modern 220S. All body types now came with unit-body construction. Coupe and convertible styling looked more modern with the separate, prewar-style fenders and running boards replaced by an up-to-date body with integrated fenders. Only the sedan was offered initially but the coupe and convertible joined the range later in '56.

Benz USA, wasn't organized for another eight years.

This 220S convertible looks like a prizewinner but it's not displayed at car shows. Instead, the cabriolet is a regular participant in parades. The back seat of the Mercedes is cramped to sit in, but it's sized just right for kids to stand up in during parades.

It is a European-market car with a back seat that folds down to hold luggage, and the owner has a set of period-correct factory luggage to fit. An unusual feature for a Fifties car are the detachable headrests.

1959 Buick LeSabre Convertible

Recent Buick commercials feature surprised individuals who exclaim "That's not a Buick!" when confronted by one of the marque's new vehicles, implying how much the brand has changed in recent years even if people's perceptions of it haven't yet. In 1959, Buick could have used the same tagline.

Events forced Buick to make sweeping changes. Chrysler Corporation's "Forward Look" cars of 1957 shook up the industry, and made GM styling look stale. Plus, Buick sales had dropped from 737,035 units in 1955 to only 240,659 in '58. That's what led to what Buick General Manager Edward T. Ragsdale called "the most revolutionary change" in Buick history.

The '59 Buicks were a complete break from the past. These were the lowest, sleekest Buicks yet. Though Buick shared GM's corporate A-body with three other divisions, it wasn't obvious except in the greenhouse area. Up front, all models sprouted canted quad headlights. The slim canted fins of the "Delta Wing" rear styling had never been seen on Buicks before and dominated the smooth, clean, and fairly dignified overall design.

Like most of the other divisions, Buick reshuffled its traditional series names. Limited hadn't been successful and the model was dropped. Roadmaster, Super, Century, and Special were respec-

tively replaced by Electra 225, Electra, Invicta, and LeSabre. LeSabre, the lowest-priced Buick, took its name from an acclaimed Harley Earl show car of 1951. The slow-selling hardtop station wagons were dropped from all series.

There were changes under the skin as well. All but the LeSabre got a new 401-cid V-8 rated at 325 horsepower; LeSabres carried over the 364-cid 250-bhp engine from '58. There was also a

new frame. A wider track and changes to suspension geometry improved handling. Air conditioning was a $430 option, and an increasing number of Buicks were sold with it. Air suspension (for the rear only) was rarely ordered.

The redesigned Buicks were well received by the press, and one magazine said the Buick was 1959's "most changed car" and that those changes were for the better. Tom McCahill of

Mechanix Illustrated was among the most enthusiastic. He raved, "This '59 Buick is one hell of a road car, with the traction of a leech," and, "In summing up, this '59 car is by far the best Buick that has ever been built."

Unfortunately, the public wasn't as enthusiastic about the revolutionary new Buick as McCahill. Buick slipped from fifth place in the market to seventh. Perhaps the '59s were too different from what Buick owners had come to expect.

LeSabre was billed as "the thriftiest Buick." For the year, Buick issued 10,489 LeSabre convertibles, with prices starting at $3129.

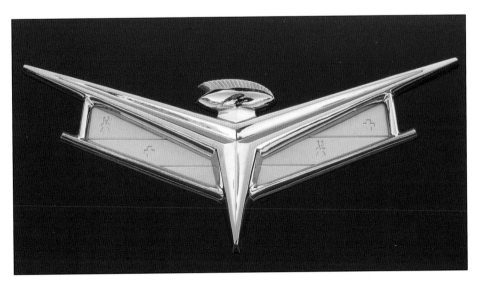

1959 Chevrolet Parkwood Station Wagon

When the 1959 Chevrolets bowed in showrooms on October 16, 1958, car shoppers could have been excused a certain amount of disbelief. Here was the brand's third different body design in as many years. Even at the height of the annual-model-change era nobody did that!

Compared with the car it replaced, this radically restyled new Chevy was longer, lower, wider, finnier—just about any "-er" that a car could be. The Impala, a flossy subseries in '58, added four-door models and became the new top of the line. Even then, however, it was impossible to change every last part of the car.

While wheelbase was stretched to 119 inches, a 1.5-inch gain, the cruciform frame design and rear coil springs that were new for 1958 were continued. Horsepower ratings were juggled, but engines were familiar: a 235-cid six and V-8s of 283 and 348 cubic inches. A four-speed manual transmission was a new option to a lineup that already

included the conventional three-speed stickshift, overdrive, and two automatics—Powerglide and the smooth but complex Turboglide.

Another similarity to 1958 was a stand-alone line of station wagons in a wide array of body, seating, and trim configurations. At the bottom sat the Brookwoods, two- and four-door six-seaters equipped on a par with the

Biscayne sedans. At the top was the Impala-like Nomad, a six-place four-door. In between were two cars with new names: the Kingswood for nine passengers and the Parkwood for six passengers, both equipped with Bel Air-type trappings.

The most fundamental change to Chevrolet's station wagons for '59 was a catch-up feature that all Chrysler

Corporation wagons had been using for the previous two years. That was a rear window that retracted into the tailgate. Gone was the traditional two-piece "clamshell" gate with an upper transom window that had to be propped open. A hideaway crank located near the top of the tailgate wound the window down into the tailgate, but for added convenience, a remote power retractor was a $32 option.

Chevy claimed that its 1959 wagons had a maximum cargo capacity of 92

cubic feet, a gain of four cubic feet from '58. With the tailgate down, the available load floor stretched to almost 10 feet in length. "You can stow a whole half-ton of gear in Chevy's roomy back end—or use it as sleeping space on overnight excursions," boasted the sales catalog.

Most wagons were fitted with a 17-gallon fuel tank—the exception being the tank in the Kingswood, which could hold one additional gallon. Station wagons and convertibles came standard with 8.00×14 tires that were slightly wider than those employed by other body styles.

The powerteam in the wagon featured here is the 185-bhp 283 with two-barrel carburetor hooked to the three-speed column-shifted manual transmission, which is what Chevrolet included in the $2867 base price of a V-8 Parkwood. As it is, this car wouldn't have gone out the door at that price, though, not with all the options and accessories installed that include power steering and brakes, a front grille guard, dual outside mirrors, side-window visors, door-handle guards, bright rocker-panel trim, spinner wheel covers, whitewall tires, and rear-window air deflectors.

Production numbers for individual wagon models are not available, but Chevy built an estimated 212,700 of all types for the model year.

1959 Chrysler New Yorker Hardtop Coupe

The smartly elegant "Forward Look" offered by Chrysler Corporation for 1955-56 hurtled into '57 with enough aesthetic force to turn Detroit auto design on its ear. What had been the stodgiest of the Big Three was suddenly the industry's design leader. Company offerings for 1957 were delta-shaped in profile: low, lean, and swoopy, and although they gave the impression of great length, they actually were a bit shorter than the '56 models.

In a Detroit era when show cars had names like Predictor and Nucleon, the

various new Chrysler products really did have an aura of futurism. A Plymouth ad line shouted, "Suddenly, it's 1960!"—and it sounded like understatement.

For the period, the Chrysler vehicles were restrained and carried the new look well. Form didn't exactly follow function, but the great fantails of fins didn't appear tacked on, either, and

chrome and side trim were reasonably simple as well.

At Chrysler Division, the New Yorker had been the top of the line off and on since just before World War II, and rode that status into the late Fifties because the Imperial that had top billing at times was spun off as its own marque for 1955.

For 1957 and '58, the New Yorker ran with a 392-cid "hemi" V-8 producing 325 or 345 bhp. The hemi had a heavy mystique, but it was expensive to produce, so for 1959 Chrysler fitted the New Yorker with a 413-cid V-8 sporting wedge-shaped combustion chambers, a four-barrel carburetor, 4.18×3.75-inch bore and stroke, and a 10.0:1 com-

pression ratio. The motor lacked only the hemi allure; in power, it was that engine's equal, and more, producing a thumping 350 horses at 4600 rpm and 470 pound-feet of torque at 2800. The sole transmission was a three-speed TorqueFlite automatic.

Front suspension brought upper A-arms, lower traverse arms, longitudinal torsion bars, and an antiroll bar. Out back was a live axle and semi-elliptic leaf springs. Brakes, front and rear, were drums.

The '59 hardtop coupe had some physical substance, weighing in at 4080 pounds but able, nonetheless,

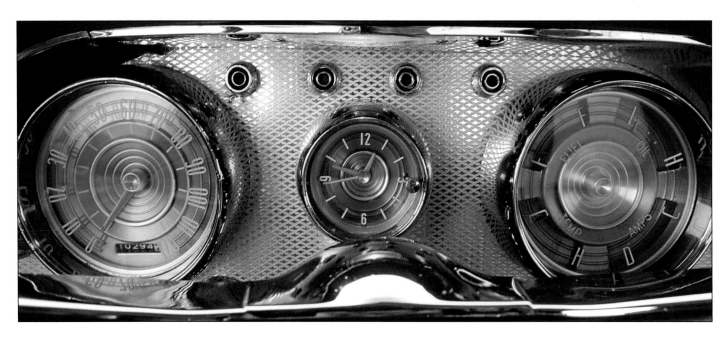

to sprint from zero to 60 in about 10 seconds. Top speed was 115 mph.

On the highway, these cars were smooth, powerful performers with spacious, airy interiors, and gave away little to Cadillac, Lincoln, or Imperial. But most every design element became a bit more baroque for 1958 and again for 1959—by which time Ford and General Motors had introduced imposing, swoopy cars of their own.

In 1959, a New Yorker hardtop coupe went out the door for $4476— up from $4347 in 1958 and $4202 in '57. Unfortunately, indifferent workmanship and a tendency to rust meant that the so-so sales figures for the 1957 Chrysler line only got worse for '58 and '59. Some 8863 New Yorker hardtop coupes were produced for 1957. For '58, the total fell to 3205 (to be fair, this was due partly to the year's serious economic recession) and suffered another tumble for '59, when just 2435 units were produced.

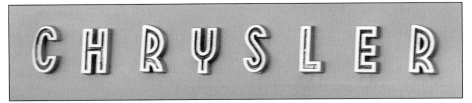

1959 Goggomobil Dart Roadster

It was an unlikely chain of events: A farm-implement company in Dingolfing, Germany, making possible a sports car produced in Punchbowl, Australia. Yet, that's the odd parentage of the Goggomobil Dart.

In Germany's devastated postwar economy, sales of the Glas sowing machine were few, but there was a need for inexpensive transportation. Glas began building scooters and then, in 1955, the Goggomobil microcar. The Goggomobil competed with cars like the BMW Isetta, and was popular for a time. Glas added larger models but by 1966 the company was in financial trouble. BMW, which needed more production capacity, purchased Glas for its factory space. The last Glas car was built in 1968.

Meanwhile, in the late Fifties, an Australian car importer was looking for an economy vehicle to add to his line. Bill Buckle signed an agreement to import Goggomobil components. The "Goggo" was built on a steel platform chassis with a 71-inch wheelbase and had independent suspension at both ends. Steering was by rack and pinion—as was popular on sports cars. Not so sporty was the tiny two-cylinder, two-stroke engine mounted in the rear of the car. The Australian Goggomobils (with locally built fiberglass bodies to reduce heavy import duties imposed on complete cars) were assembled at the Buckle Motors plant in the Sydney suburb of Punchbowl.

Buckle designed a fiberglass roadster body seemingly influenced by the Lotus Eleven racer. It was molded in upper and lower sections and joined in the middle with a rubber strip to hide the joint. Most lacked doors, although a driver's-side door was available. A Renault Dauphine rear window was used for the windshield. Being a rear-engined car, the space under the "hood" was for cargo. Buckle named the car Dart.

Two engine sizes were available: 293cc developing 15 bhp, and 393cc putting out 20 bhp. The Dart weighed only 840 pounds and was able to reach 65 mph with the larger engine. Fuel economy was said to be in the 40-45-mpg range. A four-speed manual transmission helped make the most of the meager horsepower, and provided entertaining acceleration around town.

A tight turning radius and small size also made it fun to drive in town. Overall length was only 120 inches—much smaller than the 153 inches of a 2015 Mazda Miata. In fact, its overall length was the same as the wheelbase of some full-sized American cars of the time.

The Dart was introduced in 1959, and Buckle Motors couldn't build enough of them. Then, when the Mini reached Australia in 1961, sales plummeted and Buckle ended production that year. In all, 700 Darts were built; it is estimated that only 30 to 100 survive.

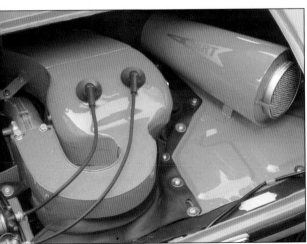

1959 Jaguar Mark IX Four-Door Sedan

During World War II, Jaguar decided to develop a dohc engine that would power sedans capable of 100 mph. Only race cars and exotics such as Duesenberg, Bugatti, and Alfa Romeo had used such a valvetrain before World War II. The twin-cam's efficient breathing allowed Jaguar's XK engine to wring 160 bhp from a 210-cid six—the same power as Cadillac's 331-cid V-8 introduced at about the same time.

Because the XK was designed to serve sedans, it was also smooth, silent, and durable. Jaguar made sure the engine looked impressive with polished-aluminum cam covers. It would be in production for 44 years.

In order to ramp up XK engine production before volume use in the sedans that paid the company's bills, the first car to get the powerplant was the XK120 sports car introduced at the 1948 London Motor Show. For 1951, Jaguar introduced the XK-powered Mark VII sedan. Styling was of the stately English school, but the Mark VII lost the prewar look of earlier Jaguar sedans. Inside, though, there was still as much wood and leather as you would find in a prewar Rolls-Royce or Bentley.

The Mark VII shared the XK120's torsion-bar independent front suspension and had good handling for a 3700-pound sedan. It had a top speed of 101 mph and did well in rallies.

Jaguar hoped that a large (by British standards), comfortable sedan with good performance would do well in the important American market. One American impressed by the Mark VII was *Road & Track* editor Bill Corey. Corey took a Mark VII on a road trip in '52 and wrote, "[W]e cruised the car at slightly under 'red-line' on the tach, about 100 miles per hour. There is no question that this is the greatest highway car your author has ever had the pleasure of driving." Corey went on to say, "[S]ome of the detours we encountered defied description. They offered a chance to break the heart of the Jag, and try we did. We drove 70 [mph] over roads that other cars could scarcely negotiate at 25. Nothing broke. Nothing happened. Not a squeak nor a rattle. Nothing."

A Mark VIII was introduced in 1956 with more power and revised styling. The Mark IX of 1959 looked virtually the same as the Mark VIII, but had several important improvements. The XK engine had grown to 231 cid (3.8 liters) and horsepower was up to 220. Top speed was now 114 mph with 0-60 mph in 11.3 seconds. To handle the extra power, Mark IXs gained four-wheel disc brakes. Power steering was standard and must have helped sales in the U.S., as did the Borg-Warner three-speed automatic transmission—standard on cars bound for America. The Mark IX was in production through 1961, when it was replaced by the longer, lower Mark X.

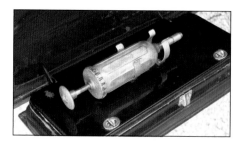

This car retains its factory tool kit. Perhaps as a comment on Jaguar reliability, an unusual collection of tools and spares was mounted in recessed compartments in the doors, including light bulbs, a spark plug, and a grease gun.

1959 Mercury Colony Park Station Wagon

The 1959 Mercury should have been more popular. Redesigned for the second time in three years, Ford Motor Company's medium-price mainstay offered the biggest, smoothest, roomiest cars in its 20-year history, plus better handling, new features, and arguably nicer styling. Yet for all that, Mercury sales skidded to a decade low of just less than 150,000. In the segment, only Chrysler, DeSoto, and ill-starred Edsel fared worse.

What happened? Basically General Motors, whose rival Buick, Oldsmobile, and Pontiac lines were unexpectedly redesigned—and in dramatic fashion. Though all three improved on their mediocre '58 sales, the handsome Wide-Track Pontiac was the big winner, jumping from sixth to fourth in the industry race on substantially higher volume of near 383,000 units. Mercury, meanwhile, slipped a notch to ninth.

Even so, the '59 "Big M" had much to recommend it. For starters, it was four inches longer, four inches wider, and three to four inches longer in wheelbase; increases made so the powertrain could sit lower and further forward in a "cow-belly" frame with siderails spread further apart. These changes resulted in a cavernous "Space-Planned" interior with a lower center tunnel, much-improved foot room, and easier entry/exit. The revised frame also allowed wider tracks for better cornering stability. Compound-curve "Panoramic Skylight" windshields enhanced the airy interior feel. So did a new slim-section dashboard with gauges and controls grouped ahead of the driver. Styling was crisper and more conservative, with pie-wedge taillamps and large, rocket-shaped bodyside sculpting the only holdovers from the "dream car" spaciness of the 1957-58 Mercury models.

Sensibly, Mercury dropped its slow-selling low-end Medalist and gaudy Turnpike Cruiser models for '59, leaving Monterey, Montclair, and luxury Park Lane hardtops, sedans, and convertibles, plus four hardtop station wagons. Colony Park remained the top-line wagon, trimmed and equipped to roughly Montclair level and distinguished by pseudo-wood body paneling. Engines again comprised 312- and 383-cid V-8s, plus a Lincoln 430 as standard and exclusive to Park Lane. All were detuned for slightly better fuel economy after the 1957-58 recession had many buyers grumbling about gas guzzlers. Automatic transmission remained mandatory, but the usual three-speed Merc-O-Matic could be newly upgraded to a more-flexible dual-range Multi-Drive unit. Both automatics were controlled by a conventional steering-column lever instead of pushbuttons, another retreat from "dream car" gimmickry.

Our featured Colony Park is one of only 5929 built, but is surely much rarer for being a pristine original. It runs the standard 322-bhp 383 V-8 and is optioned with a power tailgate window and the new front-facing third-row seat.

1959 Oldsmobile Dynamic 88 Holiday Hardtop Coupe

For 1959, General Motors originally planned to field a lineup of facelifted 1958 models. Designer Chuck Jordan's lunchtime discovery of '57 Plymouths sporting Chrysler's trendsetting "Forward Look" design one day in August 1956 changed all of that. The resulting chain of events culminated in the 1959 GM offerings that are now some of the most memorable cars of the Fifties.

Oldsmobile marketers dubbed the new styling the "Linear Look." While significantly bigger, the '59 Olds appeared leaner and cleaner than the overchromed 1958 model. Up front, parking lamps were placed between the dual headlamps at each end of a full-width grille. Tall, narrow letters spelled out "OLDSMOBILE" in the middle part of the grille, and the hood dropped

down at the center. The clean flanks were topped at the beltline with a long nacelle in place of the expected tailfin. Both of these long booms were terminated in an oval-shaped taillamp that suggested a rocket's exhaust.

Inside, occupants found a larger interior with greatly increased glass area. Passengers sat on "Fashion-Firm" seats and looked out the "Vista-Panoramic"

windshield. The "Safety-Spectrum" speedometer kept the driver informed of his speed, and, upon reaching the destination, "Easi-Grip" release levers opened the doors.

Oldsmobile offered three series: low-price Dynamic 88, midlevel Super 88, and top-shelf Ninety-Eight. All featured a new "Guard-Beam" frame that combined elements of X-type and perimeter construction. Olds claimed the "Wide-Stance" chassis was sturdier than previous designs, helped reduce vibration, and provided a quieter "Glide" ride. Eighty-Eights shared a 123-inch wheelbase, while Ninety-Eights rode a 126.3-inch span.

The Dynamic 88 had a 371-cid "Rocket" V-8 that was rated at 270 bhp with the standard "Econ-o-way" two-bar-

rel carburetor, or 300 with the extra-cost four-barrel carb. A three-speed manual transmission was standard, but the optional "Jetaway" Hydra-Matic automatic transmission was found on most cars.

Oldsmobile offered six body styles, but the Dynamic 88 was the sole series to offer all of them. The $2837 two-door sedan was the price leader, and the Celebrity sedan was the most-

affordable four-door model. In addition, there were two Holiday hardtops: the two-door SceniCoupe and the four-door SportSedan. A convertible and the four-door Fiesta station wagon rounded out the choices.

Dick Smith Oldsmobile in Melbourne, Florida, sold this Dynamic 88 Holiday SceniCoupe on April 21, 1959. Base price was $2958.

1960 Edsel Ranger Two-Door Sedan

Introduced by the Ford Motor Company in September 1957, Edsel was Ford's attempt to capture a larger portion of the medium-price new-car market. But by the start of the 1960 model year, the brand was on very shaky ground.

As the medium-price market developed in the years between the world wars, Ford really didn't do anything to address this growing—and profitable—part of the business. The 1939 Mercury was the company's first medium-price offering, but it had to compete with Pontiac, Oldsmobile, and Buick from

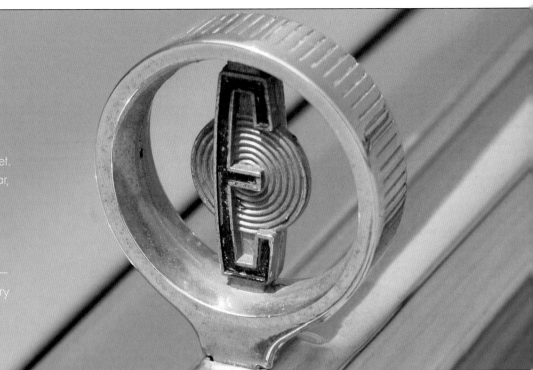

General Motors; Dodge, DeSoto, and Chrysler from Chrysler; and a collection of strong independents including Nash and Hudson.

Ford executives recognized the importance of this market soon after the end of World War II. Still, serious strategic planning didn't begin until the Fifties.

Carefully orchestrated leaks and media speculation preceded the introduction of FoMoCo's new medium-price car, the 1958 Edsel. Despite the hoopla, the Edsel faced major problems even before it ever went on sale.

The new car found itself caught up in a perfect storm of brutal office politics, a dramatic sales downturn in the medium-price field, and the worst economic

conditions since the end of World War II. With sales failing to live up to expectations from the start, and powerful opponents in company management, Edsel quickly lost support inside of Ford, even before New Year's Day 1958. It

was branded a loser, but no matter how good or bad the '58 Edsel truly was, it never really had a chance to succeed.

Edsel offerings were dramatically scaled back for 1959, and by 1960, the Edsel was little more than a badge-

engineered Ford. Introduced on October 15, 1959, the '60 Edsel arrived in one series, Ranger. Body styles included two- and four-door sedans and hardtops, a convertible, and six- and nine-passenger Villager station wagons.

Ranger

Unique sheetmetal was at a minimum, with the hood and the small sections of the rear fenders next to the decklid being the differences. Edsel's signature central vertical grille was jettisoned, and the new front end looked quite similar to a 1959 Pontiac. At the rear, vertical taillamps set the car apart from the '60 Ford with its horizontal lenses.

Response was tepid, allowing the company to throw in the towel on Edsel a little more than a month after introduction. Production ended by November 30, 1959, after a mere 2846 units.

The two-door sedan was the price leader of the line at $2643 to start, and the second-most popular 1960 Edsel model with a run of 777 units. A 292-cid V-8 with 185 bhp was standard, but the car featured here has the 223-cid "Econ-O-Six," a $83.70 credit option.

1960 Ford Galaxie Starliner Hardtop Coupe

Say this for the 1960 Ford: It was big and it certainly was bold.

Ford's all-new "standards"—a qualifier that was especially necessary now that the division was also making the personal-luxury Thunderbird and the compact Falcon—dropped every comfortably familiar marque styling cue of recent years. Instead, Ford went to a low, wide design topped off by trendy horizontal tailfins.

A broad grille that newly incorporated the quad headlights clearly demonstrated that the Fifties were over. The usual circular taillights were abandoned for roughly semicircular lenses set at either end of a concave body cove. Closed cars were topped by glassy "greenhouses" that Ford said had up to 31 percent more glass area than before. Reverse-slant "dogleg" windshield pillars, a faddish but not particularly convenient

feature of recent years, were replaced by forward-leaning pillars that eased entry and exit.

The look had originated as an advanced-design project dubbed "Quicksilver." When influential company chieftains warmed to it—by some accounts after being tipped off that rival Chevrolet was going to sweeping "batwing" fins for '59—the concept was ticketed to be the 1960 Ford.

The result was a car that was 5.6 inches longer and 4.9 inches wider than the popular 1959 Ford. Meanwhile, the '60 two-door hardtop sat an inch lower at 55 inches tall. Though the Quicksilver had been expected to ride an all-new chassis, the production 1960 Ford actually used a modified version of the marque's existing platform, albeit with the wheelbase nudged up one inch to 119.

If anything stayed the same, it was the series names. The Galaxie, which had just been introduced in '59, remained Ford's top line. It included two- and four-door sedans, a four-door hardtop, the Sunliner convertible, and a two-door hardtop newly known as the Starliner.

While other closed Galaxies kept their Thunderbird-inspired roofs with wide sail panels, the Starliner changed to thin, arcing pillars and a huge backlight, a style that was popular then. However, Ford customers didn't seem to like it as much, and it was dropped after 1961.

Here's another thing that can be said for the 1960 Fords: Some of them were lavender, or—to be exact—Orchid Gray like our featured car. It came with that year's base V-8 offering, a 292-cid powerplant. Designed to run on regular fuel with a two-barrel carb, the engine made 185 bhp. Extra-cost features on this car include Fordomatic automatic transmission, "SelectAire" air conditioner, chrome hood ornament, spotlight, fender skirts, back-up lights, and rubber-tipped rear bumper guards.

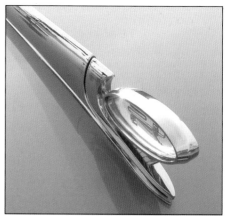

1960 Plymouth Fury Hardtop Coupe

Nineteen sixty didn't turn out the way that Virgil Exner envisioned.

Three years earlier, advertising for Plymouth proclaimed "Suddenly, it's 1960." With its low beltline, soaring tailfins, and large expanse of glass, the '57 Plymouth did look futuristic. The rest of Detroit scrambled to catch up with the "Forward Look" promulgated by Exner, Chrysler's vice president for styling. It was during these heady times that the 1960 Plymouth was styled.

However, taste changed direction abruptly, and by 1960 tailfins were on the way out. The public wanted cleaner, trimmer cars. The 1960 Plymouths were out of step with the times and sales plummeted.

That was too bad, because Plymouth had a lot going for it. Unibody construction was new that year and resulted

in a more rigid, squeak-free body. To combat Chrysler Corporation cars' rusty reputation, a seven-step rustproofing procedure was adopted. Torsion-bar front suspension was retained and Plymouth handling was superior to its Chevrolet and Ford competition. *Motor Trend* said, "The Plymouth, one of the best handling cars we tested in 1959, is even better this year." Engines ranged from a new ohv Slant Six with 145 bhp to a 383-cid "SonoRamic Commando" V-8 developing 330 horsepower and an impressive 460 pound-feet of torque.

Our featured car is equipped with the year's second most powerful V-8, the 361-cid "Golden Commando" rated at 305 bhp. *Mechanix Illustrated's* Tom McCahill reported, "A Plymouth equipped with 361 Golden Commando will run the ears off anything in its class as it comes from the showroom." McCahill recorded a 0-60-mph time of 8.2 seconds. He went on to say, "The Plymouth is my choice as the Top Buy in the low-priced field."

The featured car's ownership history starts in Sandpoint, Idaho, where the local Plymouth dealer typically gave his wife a new car every year. She liked this '60 Fury two-door hardtop so much that she kept it for 40 years. As such, it was a solid car on which to begin a restoration. It has been repainted and rechromed, and the carpeting was replaced, but seat covers preserved the original upholstery. Perhaps not surprisingly then, the car was named "Best Plymouth" at a Walter P. Chrysler Club national meet.

Among the options on the car are a record player and a rectangular steering wheel. When photographed, the owner relayed that the record player worked the one time he used it. The unusual steering wheel makes it easier to slide in and out, as well as giving a better view of the instruments, the owner explained, adding that he didn't notice the wheel's odd shape while driving. Other options are fender skirts, large "Sky-Hi" rear window, and the "Sport Deck"—a

simulated spare-wheel impression on the trunklid. "Command Seat," with a raised seatback for the driver to provide extra back and shoulder support, was standard on Furys.

But when all was said and done, the "functional stabilizer design" and "timeless good looks" Plymouth introduced for 1960 were not new enough to inflame the public with desire. Plymouth endured its third 450,000-car year in a row— far less than hoped, especially considering that the total now included the new Valiant compact.

1960 Studebaker Hawk Coupe

All '60 Studebaker Hawks had a 289-cid V-8. A two-barrel-carburetor version developed 210 bhp, while the optional four-barrel-carb engine with a dual exhaust system put out 225 horsepower. The car featured here has the more powerful engine and a Twin-Traction limited-slip differential. It also has the optional Borg-Warner three-speed automatic transmission. "I can pass anything on the road if I want to," the car's owner says of his Hawk's performance.

The Hawk body was a legacy of the 1953 Studebaker Starlight/Starliner coupe styled by industrial designer Raymond Loewy's staff, a look that many consider one of the outstanding designs of the Fifties. The body was facelifted for 1956 and gained a distinctive, upright grille. It also picked up the Hawk name. By the standards of the day, the Hawk was lightweight and reasonably sized with a European flair.

Studebaker advertised the Hawk as a sports car, although it was really more of a personal car. Engine choices consisted of an L-head six, Studebaker V-8s in two sizes, and a big 352-cid V-8 from corporate companion Packard. The heavy Packard engine was dropped after '56, replaced for 1957 by a supercharged Studebaker V-8,

and the Hawk had its best year with 19,674 produced. Studebaker was in serious financial straits in 1958, but the full Hawk line returned.

In 1959, the phenomenal success of the compact Lark saved the company. Studebaker wanted to kill the Hawk and concentrate on Larks, but dealers insisted on having something other than an economy car in their showrooms. The Hawk was saved, but on a reduced scale. The graceful hardtop was gone; only the pillared coupe remained. Engine choice was down to only the six and the smaller 259-cid V-8.

The 1960 edition of the car didn't go on sale until February of that year. The six-cylinder engine was gone (except for export cars), and the 259 V-8 was replaced by the larger 289. The standard version was good for 210 horsepower, while an optional upgrade gave 225. The Hawk's 289-cube V-8 was considered small at the time but it only had

to pull 3200 pounds (compared to 3800 pounds for a Ford Thunderbird). Performance was quite good with a top speed of 115 mph—and new finned brake drums improved stopping capability. The base price of $2650 was a good $1100 less than the starting tab for a Thunderbird. New options included a split front seat, headrests, and a tachometer. Still, Hawk demand declined to only 4507 units. For 1961, the Hawk got an optional four-speed manual transmission that made it sportier yet, but production dropped below 4000 cars.

The Hawk wasn't finished though. A thorough—and effective—Brooks Stevens facelift resulted in the Gran Turismo Hawk for 1962. Sales jumped to more than 9000 and extended the Hawk's life through early in the 1964 model year before Studebaker production was shifted to Canada for the final few years of the brand's existence.

1961 Chevrolet Corvette Convertible Coupe

Eight years removed from the Corvette's debut, the '61 model was still part of what's now called the "C1" generation—essentially 'Vettes with a straight rear axle. An all-new, flowing "ducktail" rear end, borrowed from Bill Mitchell's Stingray racer, was the 1961 Corvette's biggest change. It added luggage space as well as visual appeal. Small round taillights sat alongside the central license-plate recess, while a modest creaseline extended through the trunklid's traditional round medallion. Simple bumperettes were mounted below the taillights.

Up front, body-colored bezels helped clean up the quad-headlight nose. In addition, Corvette's trademark grille teeth were removed and replaced with a horizontal-mesh insert.

There was little different under the hood, save for a running change to a cross-flow radiator. The base powerteam that came in the $3934 starting price was a 230-bhp 283-cid V-8 hooked to a three-speed manual transmission. A four-speed manual and Powerglide automatic were alternate transmission choices. Twin-carburetor engines of 245 or 270 bhp were available, as were fuel-injected variants of 275 or 315 horsepower. Powerglide was not offered with the three hottest engine choices, and most buyers opted for the extra-cost 4-speed over the base manual. A 315-horse "fuelie" with the four-speed manual transmission could go from 0-60 mph in 5.5 seconds and top 130 mph.

Seven exterior colors were available, and the featured car is sprayed in one of the year's new ones: Fawn Beige. It is complemented with Ermine White side

coves. A Corvette fixture since 1956, the contrast-color coves would not return to the options list after '61. The extra-cost wide-whitewall tires were also putting in their final appearance this year.

The matching Fawn interior was one of three possible colors that could be paired with this paint. Passengers who settled into the two vinyl bucket seats had a little more room to themselves thanks to a newly narrowed transmission tunnel. Windshield washers and sun visors were among a handful of new standard items.

Advertisements for the 1961 Corvette tended to concentrate on "lifestyle" and driving enjoyment, but performance remained a vitally important attribute. Racing success continued at Sebring, Florida, with Corvettes taking the top three places in their class at the annual

12-hour race. It was an impressive showing considering these were near-stock Corvettes, and the top-placed car finished 11th overall against much more expensive and exotic machinery. Another Corvette won its class at the Pike's Peak hillclimb in Colorado.

Corvette's slow, steady sales climb continued in 1961. The 10,939

made—all convertibles—represented a 6.6-percent gain from 1960.

The featured car runs the standard engine with a single Carter four-barrel carb and the three-speed transmission. Options include an AM signal-seeking radio ($137.75), removable hardtop ($236.75), two-tone paint ($16.15), and whitewall tires ($31.55).

1962 Mercury Monterey S-55 Hardtop Coupe

Full-sized cars with sporty bucket seats and center consoles were all the rage in the early Sixties, with Pontiac's Grand Prix and Chevrolet's Impala Super Sport grabbing market niches. Mercury entered the field in mid 1962 with the Monterey S-55. Just as mainstream Montereys were related to the Ford Galaxie, the S-55 was Merc's version of the bucket-seat Galaxie 500/XL.

The Monterey S-55 was available as a $3488 hardtop coupe or $3738 convertible. Both rode on a 120-inch wheelbase and had a standard 292-cid V-8 of 170 bhp. Extra-cost upgrades included a 352 V-8 good for 220 bhp, 390s that generated 300 or 330 horses, and two new Marauder 406-cid V-8s with 385 or 405 ponies—the latter with triple two-barrel carbs. A Multi-Drive three-speed automatic transmission was standard; a Borg-Warner four-speed manual was optional. (Cars with either of the 406 V-8s required the four-speed and came on a 119-inch chassis with heavy-duty suspension parts.)

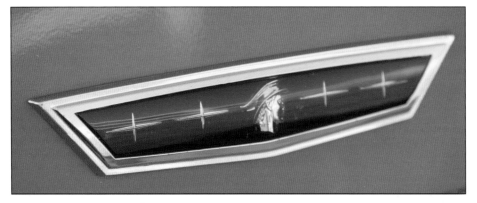

The S-55 featured unique exterior trim and a special vinyl-upholstered interior. A floor shift sprouted from the brightly trimmed console regardless of transmission choice. Only 4087 S-55s were built during its short introductory year: 2772 hardtops and 1315 convertibles.

The 1962 Mercury Monterey S-55 hardtop that's featured here may look restored, but it's an original car with 86,000 miles on the odometer. The first owner drove this car until the early Eighties when poor health forced him to store it in a garage. There it sat until 2000. The car was in excellent condition and only a good polishing was required to bring the paint back to like-new condition. The special S-55 wheel covers with distinctive red, white, and blue centers are original. The first owner always kept them in the trunk. As usual for a car awakened from a long sleep, the S-55 needed new tires, a carb rebuild, and brake-seal replacements; otherwise, it was mechanically sound.

1962 Oldsmobile F-85 Jetfire Hardtop Coupe

General Motors was flexing its engineering muscles in the early Sixties, especially when it came to the corporation's new Y-body small cars. The line of 112-inch-wheelbase premium compacts included the Pontiac Tempest with independent rear suspension and curved "rope drive" driveshaft. Meanwhile, the Buick Special and Oldsmobile F-85 bowed in 1961 with an aluminum V-8, followed in '62 by a 90-degree V-6 that was initially exclusive to Buick.

In April 1962, Oldsmobile introduced America's first mass-market turbocharged car, the F-85 Jetfire. (Chevrolet brought out its turbocharged Corvair Monza Spyder about a month later.) A turbocharger uses the force of escaping exhaust gas to turn impellers that raise air pressure in the intake manifold, forcing the fuel mixture into the combustion chambers for more power. Working with Garrett AirResearch, Olds adapted a turbocharger to the 215-cid aluminum V-8. Where the naturally aspirated versions made 155 or 185 bhp, the Jetfire's "Turbo Rocket" version put out 215 horsepower.

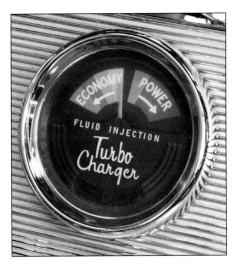

Turbo engines usually run reduced compression to avoid preignition or "pinging," but to reach the magic one-horsepower-per-cubic-inch mark, Olds engineers used a high 10.25:1 compression. To head off detonation, an ingenious fluid-injection system added a 50/50 mix of water and alcohol ("Turbo-Rocket Fluid") to the fuel mixture to lower the combustion-chamber temperature. A wastegate limited boost.

Inside, a vacuum-boost gauge on the standard center console indicated if the turbo was doing its job. The gauge also included a warning light to remind owners to refill the Turbo-Rocket Fluid tank—a bottle in the engine bay held an emergency supply.

A Jetfire could go 0-60 mph in 8.5 seconds and had a top speed of 107. The quarter-mile run was achieved in

16.8 seconds. All Jetfires were hardtop coupes with standard front bucket seats. The Jetfire cost $3049.

The ingenuity of Oldsmobile engineers made the turbo work, but ultimately the engine was unreliable in the hands of average owners who often failed to refill the Turbo-Rocket Fluid tank. In 1965 Olds recalled the Jetfires to replace the turbocharger with a conventional four-barrel carburetor. Today, computerized turbos are increasingly popular because they generate more power from small, fuel-efficient engines.

Only 3765 Jetfires were sold in 1962, with a further 5842 built in its final year of 1963. It's estimated that only 30-35 with a functioning turbocharger remain like this Chariot Red '62. It's one of only about 50 built with a four-speed manual transmission.

1962 Pontiac Bonneville Safari Station Wagon

Pontiac enjoyed a very good year in 1962. Output soared to 521,437, an increase of more than 181,000 units from 1961's tally. This total vaulted Pontiac to third in industry sales, the first time the division ranked that high. Offerings were comprised of full-sized Catalina, Star Chief, Bonneville, and Grand Prix models. The Tempest "senior compact" series rounded out the lineup.

Pontiac big-car styling evolved from the look adopted for 1961. At the front, the split-grille theme remained, but the sections featured thin horizontal bars

stacked vertically. The body-color piece that divided the grille halves thrust forward to create a peak that was flared into the hood and front bumper. Dual headlamp groups were set horizontally on each side.

On the sides, sculpturing that suggested a tube ran the full length of the body rather than tapering to points at each end. Side trim varied by series, with the most elaborate treatment reserved for Bonnevilles. Out back there was a new

bumper and C-shaped taillamps that looked like parentheses bracketing the concave cove that ran between them.

Some full-sized 1962 Pontiacs received new rooflines, but the station wagons used largely the same roof as

in '61. Wagon styling closely followed the others, but elliptical taillamps set on end and mounted on each side of the tailgate were the most obvious deviation. In addition, wagons did without the concave cove between the taillamps.

Pontiac used the Safari moniker on all of its station wagons, announced in script on the tailgate. Full-sized examples were available in Catalina and Bonneville Custom trim. Both offered a six-passenger version, and a nine-seat

Catalina was also available. All three used a 119-inch wheelbase and measured 212.3 inches long.

The Bonneville Custom Safari started at $3624, which made it the year's most-expensive Pontiac. Only 4527

were produced, the lowest total of any 1962 Pontiac model. By comparison, dealers were able to move 30,115 Catalina Safaris.

This Ensign Blue wagon was originally ordered by an AC Delco dealer from Richmond, Virginia, who selected options that brought the sticker price to more than $5400. It's one of just five '62 Safaris built with bucket seats and a console. Other extras include aluminum eight-lug wheels, air conditioning, power steering, power brakes, Safe-T-Track differential, Wonder Bar radio, tachometer, and luggage carrier. A 318-bhp 389-cid Tri-Power V-8 resides under the hood and mates to a Hydra-Matic transmission.

1963 Ford Fairlane 500 Sports Coupe

If Frank Sinatra was a Ford man, he might have sang about how 1963 was a very good year. In Dearborn, it certainly was.

At the start of the model run, Ford's four passenger-car lines wore freshened styling. For the midsized Fairlanes, the most obvious change was a front end restyled along the lines of the year's full-sized Fords. The rear fenders still wore small fins, though.

Fairlane offered only two- and four-door-sedan bodies in 1962. For its sophomore season, it added four-door station wagons and two-door hardtops.

The latter was limited to the tonier Fairlane 500 series, and was offered in two versions. For a base price of $2324, it was possible to get a Fairlane hardtop with a front bench seat.

Then there was the Sports Coupe, which added front bucket seats, a con-

sole, spinner wheel covers, and Sports Coupe script on the decklid. It was the only '63 Fairlane to wear three Buick-style "ventiports" on each front fender.

But the really big news came several months later when Ford's "half-year" model program arguably reached new heights. The basic idea was to introduce model variants and engine options partway through the selling season to reinvigorate interest.

The best remembered of Ford's "1963½" additions are almost certainly the Sports Hardtop semifastback two-door Galaxies. The legendary 427-cid V-8 was another midyear intro, and the Thunderbird Landau hardtop received a new appearance package.

The compact Falcon got in on the action with a new two-door hardtop that shared its general shape with the Gal-axie Sports Hardtop. Then, too, there was the sport-themed Sprint model and Falcon's first V-8, a 164-bhp 260-cid small-block inherited from the Fairlane.

The Fairlane was not ignored in mid-1963. While there wasn't a flashy new

model, there was the availability of a thrilling "High-Performance" 289-cid V-8 engine that was good for 271 bhp and 312 pound-feet of torque. Performance goodies on the new mill included a four-barrel carburetor, a solid-lifter cam, and header-style exhaust manifolds. Modified heads ran 11.0:1 compression. The new 289 was offered only with a four-speed manual transmission.

The "Hi-Po" 289 was a natural fit for the Fairlane, since it was the third basic version of the 221-cube small-block V-8 that Ford conjured up for the model's introduction in 1962.

The 289 could move a Fairlane from zero to 60 mph in less than nine seconds. A 289-powered hardtop starred in one '63 ad with the tagline "Wait till you feel Fairlane's Sunday Punch!"

The 271-horse 289 is probably best known for being available in the most successful of all half-year Fords, the "1964½" Mustang. Thus, it's a bit ironic that the engine first appeared as one of the least-known '63½ additions.

The 1963 Fairlane 500 Sports Coupe featured here has the 271-horse 289/four-speed power team. New, the Fairlane priced out at $3415.30.

1963 Volkswagen Type 34 Karmann-Ghia

In the late Nineties, Volkswagen tickled the automotive world's fancy when it brought out the New Beetle that called to mind the iconic shape of the round little car that put VW on the map. However, there was a time many years earlier when new-car buyers and industry observers thought that a different "new" Beetle had arrived.

That was in 1961, when Volkswagen introduced the 1500. Like its world-renowned forebear, it had an air-cooled rear-mounted four-cylinder engine, four-speed transmission, "backbone" chassis, and 94.5-inch wheelbase. Where it was supposed to be "new and improved" was with increased passenger room and more power.

There was one more thing that the 1500 had in common with the original Bug: a deluxe coupe known as the Karmann-Ghia that shared the engineering of the workaday sedans but was dressed more stylishly. However, just as the 1500 never fully took over as a replacement for the Type 1 Beetle, neither did its take on the Karmann-Ghia become as popular as its original namesake. This was particularly true in the U.S., where the 1500 K-G was never officially imported.

All this history is what makes this Beryl Green 1963 Karmann-Ghia such a distinctive sight. Like any of these cars that has come to America, it had to arrive somewhat by chance. The car's original owner was a United States Air Force pilot who bought it when stationed in Nuremberg, Germany, and brought it home with him when he returned to the States in 1973.

The design of the Type 34 Karmann-Ghia, as the car was designated, is attributed to Sergio Sartorelli of the

coachbuilder Ghia in Turin. He opted for a light, airy roofline with better rear headroom than the older Type 14 K-G. The design's most distinctive—perhaps most polarizing—feature was an aggressive "scowling" look up front.

The 1500 series—which has alternately come to be known as the Type 3—had a more compact flat-four engine than the Beetle. As launched, the 1.5-liter powerplant generated 54 SAE-rated bhp. During 1963 came a twin-carburetted "S" version good for 66 bhp and top-speed potential of about 85 mph. It's this engine that powers the featured car.

1964 Ford Galaxie 500 Four-Door Sedan

When this Galaxie's owner answered the classified ad in a hobby publication, he thought he was buying a whistle-clean daily driver. What he wound up with was a rather unlikely

"trailer queen," a 1964 Ford Galaxie 500 four-door sedan that gets the royal treatment because the owner decided he wants to keep the odometer reading below 1000 miles.

That's right, this Wimbledon White-over-Rangoon Red 1964 Galaxie has just 920 miles on it. With a few minor exceptions, it's an homage to originality and preservation.

At the time of purchase, the car had a mere 905 miles on the odometer. Only

the original battery and fanbelt had been replaced by earlier owners. The 15 miles the Galaxie has accumulated since were mostly added in the increments necessary to move it around the shop or show fields. In his care, only the engine pulleys and a leaking heater core have been replaced. Though they're showing signs of age, the bias-ply tires are the same ones that have been on the car since it left the factory.

Full-sized 1964 Fords were at the end of a four-year styling cycle. However, that didn't prevent the designers from going all-out to make the full-sizers look fresh and new. In addition, the popularity of "slantback" hardtops prompted a "faster" roofline for two- and four-door sedans that had a bit more of a forward slope than the Thunderbird-inspired unit of recent years.

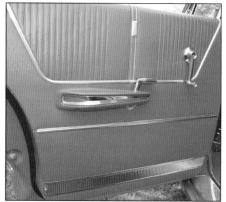

Under the reworked sheet metal, wheelbase stayed pat at 119 inches. Leaf springs supported the rear of big Fords for the last time.

With five body styles, the Galaxie 500 series offered the broadest availability of models and was the volume leader among "standard" Fords. The Galaxie 500 Town Sedan—company nomenclature for a four-door sedan— accounted for 198,805 orders, making it second only to the Galaxie 500 two-door hardtop's nearly 207,000 orders for the affections of Ford customers that year.

This age-defying car comes pretty close to depicting a Galaxie 500 Town

Sedan in its $2667 base state. Black-wall tires, Ford-lettered hubcaps, and a three-speed column-shift manual transmission were all standard-equipment items in 1964.

The handful of extra-cost options found on this Galaxie starts with its 289-cid V-8 engine. With a two-barrel carburetor and 9.0:1 compression, it develops 195 bhp at 4400 rpm. As a replacement for the standard 223-cube inline six, it added $109 to the sticker price and was just the first of several available V-8s that ran all the way to a 425-horse 427-cube job. Other add-ons to the featured car include two-tone paint, AM radio, and seat belts.

1964 Rambler American 440H Hardtop Coupe

By the time the redesigned 1964 Rambler American went on sale, the model had become an important product for American Motors.

The original American bowed in January 1958 as a smaller, lower-priced addition to Rambler's product line. Lack-ing the funds to develop an all-new car, American Motors took the unusual step of resurrecting the 100-inch-wheelbase Nash Rambler that had gone out of production in 1955. At first, only a modestly updated two-door sedan was available. Still, the American sold well, body styles and trim levels were added, and it was reskinned for 1961.

The first truly new American was the 1964 model. It was a larger, roomier car built on a 106-inch wheelbase. To save on tooling and manufactur-ing costs, the new body shared many

stampings and other components with American Motors' new-for-1963 Classic and Ambassador.

The smooth styling was handled by Richard Teague. A full selection of body styles was available: two- and four-door sedans, two-door hardtop and convertible, and four-door station wagon. Base 220 and midlevel 330 models were available in both sedan styles, and as wagons. Top-line 440s came as hardtops, convertibles, and four-door sedans. A sportier, better-equipped 440H version of the hardtop rounded out the line.

American engines were all sixes. The old 90-bhp "flathead" version of the 195.6-cid engine was standard on the 220 and 330 series. An ohv conver-

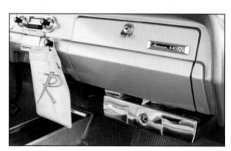

sion of the same engine rated at 125 horsepower was standard on 440s and optional on the lower-line Americans.

The top choice was a 138-horsepower version of the ohv engine with a two-barrel carburetor. It was standard on the 440H and optional on all other Americans. A total of six three-speed manual and automatic transmissions were available.

The 1964 American was popular and production reached 160,321 units. This compared to 105,296 of the 1963s. In fact, '64 would prove to be the best year that the American would ever have. While Rambler dealers sold 19,495 American 440 hardtops, the pricier 440H didn't do too badly for itself with orders of 14,527.

1966 Mercury Park Lane Convertible

Nineteen sixty-six was a facelift year for the full-size Mercury, which had been completely redesigned from the frame up in 1965 and dressed in new styling that was advertised as being "in the Lincoln Continental tradition." Still, there was enough new to give prospective customers plenty to think about.

Naturally, as was the custom in those days, appearances were freshened while still keeping within the basic styling direction selected for '65. The grille, hood, and fenders were changed, and wraparound taillights replaced the enveloped style used previously. Reshaped bumpers actually led to a two-inch gain in overall vehicle length on non-station wagon models.

Inside, gauge faces were changed to white from black. This being the year that federally mandated safety equipment started showing up in abundance, Mercurys now sported a padded dashboard and sun visors, front and rear seatbelts, four-way hazard flashers, and back-up lights.

Other new engineering advancements included larger-diameter standard drum brakes, optional front disc brakes, minor suspension tuning, and adoption of a larger 25-gallon fuel tank. Station wagons came with Ford Motor Company's new two-way tailgate that could be dropped down in the customary way for cargo loading or opened from the side for easier passenger access.

The sporting S-55 two-door hardtop and convertible returned to the line for the first time since 1963. Otherwise, the lineup continued to consist of the entry-level Monterey, step-up Montclair, premium Park Lane, and Commuter and Colony Park wagons.

The Park Lane nameplate was enjoying a second life. First used from 1958 to 1960 on the highest-priced Mercs, it made a comeback in 1964. For '66, Park Lane shoppers had a choice of

two- or four-door hardtops, a four-door sedan with the distinctive retractable reverse-angle Breezeway backlight, or a convertible. Starting prices ranged from $3387 for the hardtop coupe to $3608 for the convertible. As the costliest Park Lane, the convertible was among the rarest big Mercurys of the year—2446 were built, approximately 1.5 percent of overall production.

Park Lanes got a new standard engine, a Mercury-exclusive 410-cid V-8. With a four-barrel carburetor and single exhaust, it made 330 bhp at 4600 rpm and 444 pound-feet of torque at 2800 rpm. A three-speed manual gearbox was standard; Multi-Drive Merc-O-Matic automatic cost extra.

The original-condition Park Lane soft top featured here has an extensive complement of extra-cost comforts and conveniences, starting with the Multi-Drive automatic transmission and dual exhausts. Other optional features include power windows, door locks, and six-way front seat. Interior comfort is further enhanced by a tilt steering wheel. The car is painted in metallic Emberglo, one of 10 new colors (out of a total of 17) available for 1966 Mercurys.

1966 Plymouth Valiant Signet Hardtop Coupe

Like all the domestic economy compacts that hit the American market in the early Sixties, the Plymouth Valiant soon added sportier hardtop and convertible models. Like all the compacts that eventually spawned racier "ponycars," the Valiant's bucket-seats-and-bright-trim jobs were quickly ignored.

The Valiant's splashiest version was the Signet, a name first applied to the Plymouth compact in 1962. The next year brought a complete restyle to the Valiant with fuller lines and the addition of a pair of convertibles, one of them a Signet. The big news for '64 was a 273-cid V-8 option, but that was

overshadowed by the springtime arrival of the Barracuda fastback. Aside from its big sloping rear window, the Barracuda's visual and mechanical links to the Valiant were inescapable, and shoppers who wanted a racy small Plymouth flocked to it. The Valiant would press on with further facelifts of the 1963-vintage body through 1966—maintaining the Signet hardtop and convertible along

the way—but the all-new, sedan-only '67 Valiant would mark a return to the line's workaday economy roots.

The lightly restored '66 Signet seen here is one of 13,045 hardtops made (down from a high of 37,736 for '64). Unchanged since '63 was its 106-inch wheelbase. Also continued was a suspension set-up with front torsion bars and rear leaf springs.

Styling still featured a single headlamp per side, but they were moved inside new straight-edged front fenders. A newly flush three-element grille featured a body-color section in the center. Rear roof pillars were straightened up a bit, and the rear window glass was enlarged. The decklid and bumpers were changed too. Signets featured all-vinyl upholstery and added a wide band of

argent accent paint low on the body-sides for '66.

For power, Valiants began with a 170-cid ohv "Slant Six" hooked to a three-speed manual transmission. This Signet runs with the extra-cost 145-bhp 225-cube six and TorqueFlite automatic transmission. When *Motor Trend* tested a '66 Signet hardtop with that same combination, it went 0-60 mph in 13.6

seconds and turned a 19.5-second quarter-mile. "The Plymouth Valiant Signet doesn't offer tire-smoking acceleration, but it does deliver decent performance for normal driving—and does it with an eye to economy," said *MT*, which noted 20-plus-mpg fuel mileage.

Aside from the engine/transmission combo that would have jacked up the $2261 Signet hardtop starting price, this car counts factory air conditioning, an AM radio, bucket seats, and whitewall tires among its complement of optional equipment. The car's Soft Yellow paint has been resprayed.

1966 Volvo 122S Two-Door Sedan

Volvo has a history that stretches back to its first car in 1927. (The word "Volvo" is Latin for "I roll.") The first Volvo ÖV4 was a simple, sturdy four-cylinder car designed to appeal to the Swedish middle class. Volvo also built taxis, trucks, buses, and tractors that provided most of the company's prewar income.

Early Volvo styling was certainly influenced by American cars. The PV36 resembled a Chrysler Airflow. Volvo's postwar economy car, the PV444, was compared to a shrunken 1946 Ford.

The PV444 was a success both in Sweden and in export markets—gaining a foothold in America. Volvo wanted to build on its success with a return to the medium-price range with a larger, more expensive model. The Amazon was introduced to the Swedish market in 1957,

and American exports started in late '59. The Amazon name was licensed by a German motorcycle maker, so outside of Sweden the car was known as the 121 or 122, depending on the engine. Power was provided by the PV444's 1.6-liter four. That engine grew to 1.8 liters in 1960.

All American imports had the 122S engine with dual British SU carbs good for 90 bhp. It was a conventional ohv unit but ruggedly built with five main bearings. *Car and Driver* said, "Volvo's B-18 4-cylinder engine may be the closest thing to an unbreakable production powerplant ever developed." *CD* went on to say that the 109-cid four had more

total bearing area than a Chevy 409 V-8. Performance wasn't in the 409's league, but a 0-60-mph time of 14.9 seconds and top speed of 95-100 mph was actually quite respectable for a family compact of the Sixties.

Road tests of the time noted some body lean but considered handling stable and steering precise. Volvo was building its reputation for safety with padded dashboards and the first three-point safety belts. Not surprising for a car built near the Arctic Circle, the 122S was hailed for having one of the most powerful heaters available.

Styling was conservative, but pleasing. Again the American influence was evident, and some falsely accused Volvo of buying the body dies of the defunct Aero-Willys. The unibody structure was sturdy and had better rustproofing than most cars of the era.

The owner of the featured car has known it for nearly his entire life. In fact,

this very car was used to bring him home from the hospital as a newborn.

His father bought the 1966 Volvo 122S new and drove it 92,300 miles in a decade. He then parked the Volvo in his garage and stored it there for the next 28 years.

Before turning the Volvo over to his son, a local repair shop in New Jersey was enlisted to get the long-dormant car running again. This was followed by an adventurous road trip to its new home in northern Illinois.

Since then, the sturdy Volvo has been repainted and the interior was retrimmed with vinyl upholstery from the original Swedish supplier. Living up to Volvo's reputation for dependability, the engine has not been rebuilt and we are told it never burns a drop of oil.

1967 BMW 2000C Hardtop Coupe

BMW as we know it today began with the "New Class" 1500 introduced in 1962. The 1500 was a compact four-door sedan with a 100.5-inch wheelbase. The chassis was a clean-sheet design. Up front, there were MacPherson struts. Out back, an improved version of the semi-trailing arm and coil-spring independent rear suspension that had originally been designed for the BMW 600 and 700 was used. Other mechanical items included worm-and-roller steering and power-assisted front-disc/rear-drum brakes.

The 1500 was powered by a 1.5-liter ohc four-cylinder engine—the M10—that liked to rev and also proved durable. It was rated at 75 horsepower and mated to a 4-speed manual transmission.

The 1500 was well received in Germany, and the county's automotive press thought it filled the market niche once occupied by the well-regarded Borgward Isabella.

BMW's U.S. distributor, Max Hoffman, started imports in time for the 1963 model year. The East Coast port-of-entry price was $3550. *Road & Track* tested an early example for the September 1963 issue and concluded, "No car is perfect, but in the case of the BMW 1500, the effort of its designers and builders to approach perfection as nearly as possible within their limitations is pleasingly evident."

BMW expanded on its success with more powerful 1800 and 2000 variations on this winning theme. Then a shorter, lighter 2002 two-door sedan came out with even better performance than the four-door, and established BMW as the builder of "ultimate driving machines." The 2002 gave way to the

iconic first-generation "E21" 3 Series in the mid Seventies.

In between these two developments, a graceful 2000 coupe was introduced during 1965. The 2000 shared the sedan's mechanical components and wheelbase, but had its own sheetmetal, which was formed by coachbuilder Karmann. The 2000 was designed for style and luxury rather than outright performance, and was actually 65 pounds heavier than the sedan. It used the largest 1990cc version of the M10 engine, and was offered in two states of tune. The 2000C used a single Solex carburetor and developed 100 bhp, while the

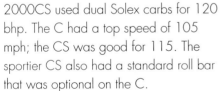

2000CS used dual Solex carbs for 120 bhp. The C had a top speed of 105 mph; the CS was good for 115. The sportier CS also had a standard roll bar that was optional on the C.

BMW added a more powerful six-cylinder version of the coupe in 1968. It immediately outsold the 2000C/CS fours, which were dropped after 1969. Today, the 2000 coupe is a rare car in the U.S.

The restored 1967 2000C on these pages wears flush European-style headlights rather than the exposed sealed-beam quad headlights originally required on American-market cars.

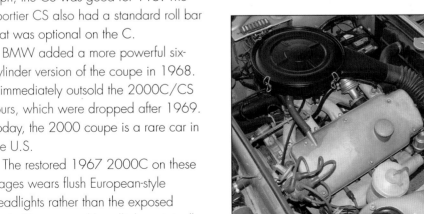

1968 Kaiser Jeep
Jeepster Convertible

By the mid Sixties, Jeep's dominance of the then-small four-wheel-drive market was being challenged by the International Scout and the Ford Bronco. To retaliate, Kaiser Jeep Corporation went Commando.

Its new Jeepster Commando line bowed for 1967 with modern, slab-

sided styling and more carlike creature comforts than Jeep's CJ series. Steel doors and roll-up windows were standard. Jeepster was also smaller and more affordable than Jeep's Wagoneer. A sport-utility-vehicle market was beginning to develop, and Jeep now had two strong contenders.

The Commando line started with the $2466 roadster, a $2548 pickup, and a $2749 station wagon. The most expensive Jeepster was the convertible

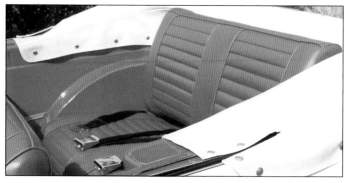

at $3186. The convertible dropped the Commando name from its handle, but added two-tone paint and a "Continental" spare tire. Inside were vinyl bucket seats, vinyl-trimmed door panels, and a simple car-type instrument panel. The stylish convertible was the spiritual successor to the rear-drive Willys Jeepster Phaeton of 1948-51. Although attractive, the first Jeepster was expensive and proved a slow seller. The new Jeepster was reasonably priced—especially with standard four-wheel drive. Initial advertising appealed to youth and pitched the Jeepster as a sporty vehicle that could go anywhere. The ad headline usually started with "Holy Toledo," a reference to Jeep's factory in Toledo, Ohio.

Under the new sheetmetal was a 101-inch-wheelbase chassis from the CJ-6, a longer version of the Jeep CJ-5. The standard engine was the venerable "Hurricane" F-head four with 75 bhp, but the optional 155-bhp "Dauntless" V-6 was needed for good performance. *Car Life* tested a V-6 Jeepster and recorded a 0-60-mph time of 12.6 seconds with a top speed of 87 mph—respectable figures for a vehicle with off-road capability. The optional 225-cid V-6 was originally a Buick engine, but

General Motors sold the tooling to Kaiser Jeep in time for Jeepster installation. (After the OPEC oil embargo, Jeep's new parent company, American Motors, sold the tooling back to GM, where it evolved into the popular 3800 V-6.)

For 1968, the convertible gained a hinged tailgate and a revised top. The price rose to $3442. Only 422 Jeepster convertibles were built that year.

The featured Jeepster has the optional V-6 mated to a three-speed GM Turbo Hydramatic 400 automatic transmission. The owner loves driving his Jeepster— usually with the top down. He reports that it handles well for a four-wheeler and the engine has more than adequate power. Because of the "odd-fire" V-6's unevenly spaced firing impulses, the engine is rough at idle, but smooths out once moving and it cruises comfortably at 65 mph, he says.

The Jeepster was a success with 77,573 units built (an average of about 11,000 a year) by the time production ended in 1973. A larger Wagoneer-derived Cherokee replaced it for '74. While the Cherokee proved to be a stronger seller than the Jeepster, it could never match the dash of a Jeepster convertible.

1970 Jaguar XJ6 Four-Door Sedan

Jaguar's XJ is one of the longest running model names in the industry. The XJ made its debut in September 1968 as a 1969 model, and Jaguar's flagship sedan is still badged XJ today.

There is good reason why a Jaguar sedan launched in the late Sixties should give birth to such a long-lived name. At its introduction, the XJ set a new standard for European luxury sedans.

The press raved. In the UK, *Motor* said, "We believe that in its behavior it gets closer to overall perfection than any other luxury car we have tested, regardless of price. The car just floats round

corners with such enormous reserves of adhesion that the driver's nerve will invariably be lost before the grip." In the U.S., *Road Test* exclaimed, "The Jaguar XJ6 also just happens to be the best riding car we have ever driven, and its ride/handling ratio is not equaled by any other car we can think of." *Road & Track* deemed the XJ "uncannily silent, gloriously swift, and safe as houses."

Many of the components of the new XJ were familiar. The XK 4.2-liter six-cylinder engine had been launched in 1948. It was an advanced dohc design that had powered five Le Mans winners and yet was smooth and durable. Emissions standards were starting to cut the power of the 20-year-old design, but its 245 bhp provided good performance—*Road & Track* claimed the top

speed was 124 mph, with 0-60 mph in 10.1 seconds. Its independent rear suspension had been introduced in the E-Type and Mark X in 1961.

Meanwhile, the body was all new. It used unitary construction with the suspension carried by rubber-mounted sub frames to isolate road shock and vibration. The firewall was double skinned to keep engine noise out of the cabin.

Just as the XJ's engineering received great acclaim, styling also drew praise. Jaguar's founder, Sir William Lyons, gained renown for his styling of the XK120 and E-Type sports cars. The XJ

was perhaps his best sedan design. The look of the original XJ was so successful that Jaguar used variations of the theme through 2009. Inside were the wood and leather expected of a Jaguar. The dashboard followed the E-Type layout with a comprehensive array of gauges and a long row of rocker switches.

Demand was high for the XJ6, but production was slow to get moving, and labor unrest was a constant problem. In England, the wait for delivery was soon more than 12 months. Indeed, supply and reliability would be persistent challenges for the XJ.

Still, the inherent good qualities of the XJ kept the original design in production through 1992. Along the way, a V-12-powered XJ12 was added. There were Series II and Series III updates as well. A totally new XJ6—albeit with styling that echoed the original—came out in 1986. However, its engine bay was too narrow take the V-12, so the Series III XJ12 remained in production until 1992.

Our featured 1970 Jaguar XJ6 is from the first year of American imports. It is equipped with a Borg-Warner three-speed automatic transmission, which came standard on U.S.-bound XJs.

1971 Fiat 500L
Two-Door Sedan

Prior to its global alliance with Chrysler—a partnership that commenced in mid-2009 and eventually resulted in the formation of Fiat Chrysler Automobiles—Italian automaker Fiat was a marginal player in the American auto market that nonetheless had a long history on these shores. Within a few years of Fiat's founding in 1899, its cars were already being sold in America. By 1910, most Fiats sold here were manufactured in a purpose-built plant in Poughkeepsie, New York, but production ceased during World War I and never resumed. Following the "Great War," imports returned, only to be sidetracked for a few years by World War II. Finally, after the 1983 model year, the company stopped selling Fiat-branded cars in the United States.

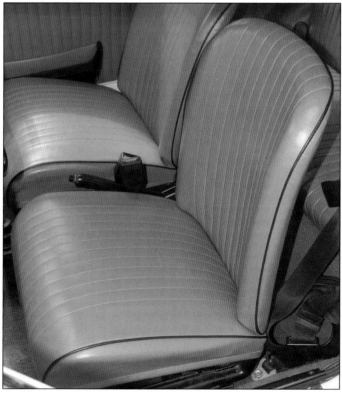

Now Americans can once again buy a Fiat, since the subcompact 500 went on sale as a 2012 model. Today's 500 pays homage to Dante Giacosa's iconic Fiat Nuova 500 that was introduced in July 1957. Giacosa also designed the original Fiat 500—the "Topolino"—of 1936. His Fifties cinquecento—Italian for 500—followed the rear-engine, rear-drive design formula that had become increasingly popular for European small cars of the era.

The 500 was very small, with a 72.4-inch wheelbase and an overall length of 116 inches. Curb weight was only 1036 pounds. The engine was a 29.2-cid air-cooled inline twin that Fiat claimed was good for 13 horsepower and returned 52.3 miles per gallon. The transmission was a nonsynchronized four-speed manual. Top speed was about 53 mph.

The front compartment housed the gas tank, battery, spare tire, and a bit of luggage space. The simple interior was said

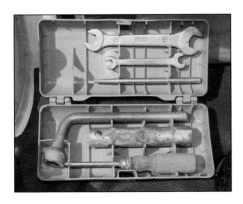

to offer comfortable seats and adequate room—at least for the two people in the front. On early versions, all glass but the front windows was fixed in place; the standard fabric roof rolled back for additional ventilation. A May 1958 advertisement in *Road & Track* pegged the 500's U.S. price at $1098.

The cinquecento's last year on the American market was 1961. The example featured here is a 1971 Fiat 500L, a version that included an upgraded interior and chrome tubular bumper guards. Originally sold in Italy, the 500L used a 22-bhp engine good for a top speed of about 75 mph. It was built from 1968 to 1972.

1971 Toyota Celica ST Hardtop Coupe

In 1971, Toyota introduced its Celica sport coupe, a car that many automotive magazines compared to the original Ford Mustang. By 1971, Mustang had grown eight inches longer and 600 pounds heavier than the '65 original. (Ford President Lee Iacocca realized this was too big for a "ponycar" and had a much smaller Mustang in the pipeline.) Meanwhile, import coupes such as

the Celica, Opel Manta, and Mercury Capri catered to those who wanted a sporty car that was smaller than the early Seventies ponycars.

Indeed, *Motor Trend*'s review of the first Celica was filled with Mustang references such as, "Yup. Somewhere, somehow, a Japanese auto maker went and pulled a real sneakie—designing a car that is so apple-pie American—and amazing like the first Mustang—that it could fit in just anyplace—not just California where those nutballs will drive anything to be different."

Toyota was building a reputation for dependable sedans, though it had built a few sports cars such as the tiny Sports 800 and the limited-production 2000GT. The Celica was Toyota's first volume sport coupe. It was powered by a 113.4-cid (1.9-liter) ohc four-cylinder engine that developed 108 bhp. A four-speed manual transmission was standard, as were front disc brakes. The notchback two-door hardtop rode on a 95.5-inch wheelbase; its curb weight was a reasonable 2290 pounds. The base price was also reasonable at $2598. Sales in the U.S. were brisk with more than 17,000 sold the first year. Celica found a niche in the American market and successive generations of the nameplate were sold through 2005.

In its first exposure to the Celica, *Motor Trend* was impressed with the styling, interior, comprehensive standard equipment, and build quality. The long hood and short rear deck were reminiscent of an American ponycar. The interior was well executed with reclining bucket seats, nylon carpet, and full instrumentation. *MT* found the performance acceptable, with 0-60 mph in 12.7 seconds, but was less impressed with handling. "How does the Celica handle? Disappointingly for a car that's being touted as a 'sports tourer,' but good as a replacement for the original Mustang." One problem was a nose-heavy 59-percent-front/41-percent-rear weight distribution. Another was the small 13-inch wheels with narrow 165SR13 tires.

Our featured car was the 13th Celica built for the U.S. market. Its owner says the vintage Celica is a nice car that you can enjoy driving, yet is practical.

He claims the Celica is a typical Seventies car: a little underpowered, but "light" to drive with good steering and brakes. The featured car didn't require a full restoration, just little things and paint. It wears a set of Minilite alloy wheels that are a period-correct aftermarket accessory that complement the sporty styling of the Celica.

1972 AMC Gremlin X Two-Door Sedan

American Motors positioned itself as the nation's small-car leader. AMC knew it couldn't compete head to head in every segment with the Big Three, but money could be made in the compact field, where they typically showed little interest. In the late Sixties, AMC learned

that both General Motors and Ford were planning to bring out subcompact import-fighters for 1971. American Motors needed to defend its turf.

AMC was more cash strapped than usual with the development costs for the compact Hornet and the impending

purchase of Kaiser Jeep. The solution came not from the engineering department, but from styling. Styling chief Dick Teague was used to operating on tight budgets. He learned the trick of creating new looks for old body shells during the final years of Packard. Now Teague urged building a shortened version of the Hornet.

The Hornet then in development had

309

AMC's most up-to-date engineering. By lopping off 18 inches from the rear, the compact Hornet became the subcompact Gremlin, and AMC had a new model for very little investment.

The front half of the car was very much a Hornet. The difference was in the back. The rear looked as if it had been guillotined, and that was its appeal. Love it or hate it, the Gremlin got attention. The chopped rear end was also practical. It provided good cargo room, and the large hatch window was a convenience rarely seen in America at the time.

Inside the car there was also a marked difference between front and rear. The front seat retained its Hornet dimensions, and was wide and roomy for a subcompact. However, back-seat passengers knew where those 18 inches of length were cut. *Car and Driver* said "rear legroom is tighter than Nixon's fiscal policy."

Beneath the sheetmetal, engineering shortened the Hornet's wheelbase from 108 inches to 96. Tried-and-true AMC sixes provided the power (though a V-8 and a four would be added in later years). Fuel economy was in the 20-25 mpg range—not an import beater, but quite good for a domestic.

The Gremlin debuted on April Fool's Day, 1970—beating the Chevrolet Vega and Ford Pinto to market by half a year. Prices started at $1879 for a Gremlin without a back seat.

Our featured car is a 1972 Gremlin with only 27,000 original miles that still wears its original paint. It has the X package that includes body stripes, slotted steel wheels, an upgraded interior with carpeting and vinyl bucket seats, and sport steering wheel. The black paint is a rare optional color. Power is from a 232-cid (3.8-liter) six with 135 bhp. The transmission is an optional Chrysler-built Torque-Command three-speed automatic.

1972 Oldsmobile Ninety-Eight Regency Hardtop Sedan

Both Oldsmobile and Cadillac celebrated anniversaries in 1972, Cadillac its 70th and Oldsmobile—then the oldest surviving American automaker—its 75th. Both decided it was the velour anniversary. The fabric had vanished from car interiors after World War II, but thanks to the lead of Olds and Cadillac, velour became the number-one upholstery choice for American cars in the Seventies.

Oldsmobile's velour seat had a pillowed effect that made it look like an extremely inviting couch. This plush-sofa look was also widely copied during the Seventies. Olds had just created the exuberant luxury that Americans of that era craved.

This trendsetting interior made its debut in the Ninety-Eight Regency four-door hardtop, a midyear model with a production run limited to 5000 copies for '72. Tiffany & Co., the New York jeweler, styled the face of the Regency's dashboard clock and provided a sterling-silver key ring. Every Regency was sprayed in Tiffany Gold metallic paint, but the interior was available in a choice of black or gold.

Olds realized it was on to a good thing and brought back the Regency as a regular model for '73, selling more than 34,000 of them. The name would remain a part of the Ninety-Eight family until the end of that line in 1996, after which it transferred to the Eighty-Eight range through '98.

John Beltz, Oldsmobile's general manager from 1969 to 1972, said Olds buyers didn't want small cars, and the Ninety-Eight certainly wasn't, not with a 127-inch wheelbase and an overall length of 228 inches. Beltz also said it

was much easier to reduce emissions in a big engine because it was usually operating at only part throttle. Of course, he said this before the 1973-74 OPEC oil embargo, when most Americans weren't yet overly concerned with fuel economy. The Ninety-Eight had a 455-cid 250-bhp V-8 to move its 4698 pounds, and it moved them well. A '71 Ninety-Eight did 0-60 mph in 8.7 seconds (but averaged only 11 mpg) in *Motor Trend* testing.

The Regency pictured here was purchased new by an elderly lady who drove it only 12,288 miles and kept it in an air-conditioned garage. Thanks to gentle use, it remains in like-new condition. Only tires, battery, and belts have been replaced. The rest is original. Options include an eight-track tape player and an external temperature gauge mounted outside on the driver's door.

1973 Ford Gran Torino Sport SportsRoof Hardtop Coupe

Among intermediate-class cars, the Torino had been running second in sales to Chevrolet's Chevelle prior to 1972. The redesigned '72 Torino was larger and more like full-sized Fords than the previous generation. A traditional perimeter frame isolated from the separate body by rubber body mounts replaced unibody construction. This, plus a redesigned suspension, resulted in a smoother ride. All Torinos had standard front disc brakes—a rarity in the early Seventies.

The Torino buyer could choose a hardtop coupe, four-door sedan, or station wagon in base or Gran Torino trims. Gran Torinos had nicer interiors and a more distinctive grille. The Gran Torino Sport was the performance line, offered as a notchback hardtop coupe or as a "SportsRoof" fastback that was unique to the Sport series. All Gran Torino Sports were V-8 powered. The bigger, better-riding Torino with attractive new styling was a hit and production increased by 52 percent over 1971—more than

enough to put Torino well ahead of archrival Chevelle.

The biggest change for 1973 was a new front end designed to meet the federal requirement that cars withstand a five-mph crash without damage. A flat front end with a girderlike bumper replaced Torino's sculpted sheetmetal. Engines lost power as emissions standards tightened. The engine choices for the Gran Torino Sport ranged in size from a 302-cid V-8 with 137 bhp up to a 219-bhp 460 V-8 that was added

midyear. The most powerful engine was the four-barrel "Cleveland" 351 with free-flowing heads that allowed it to produce more horsepower than the larger V-8s. The Sport came in the same two body styles, but the SportsRoof, of which 51,853 of the '73s were made, put in its final appearance.

In spite of federal restrictions and competition from a wholly redesigned Chevelle, Torino sales for 1973 were almost the same as the previous year, and Ford remained the midsize leader.

The owners of the featured 1973 Ford Gran Torino Sport fastback coupe realized it was special when they bought it new. Today, though, it's no longer a daily driver, and it can most often be seen at car shows.

The engine is a Cleveland 351-cid V-8 with a four-barrel carburetor rated at 246 net bhp. The car is well equipped with air conditioning, AM/FM radio, Rim Blow deluxe steering wheel, rally instrument group, and Magnum 500 sports wheels.

Most Gran Torino Sports were ordered with bucket seats, but the featured car has a front bench. Also unusual is its black paint, which was a rarely seen optional color. Another unusual feature is the single flat mirror with a chromed base and body. Gran Torino Sports should have dual aerodynamic body-colored "sport" mirrors, but this is an early production car built before the sport mirrors were available from the supplier.